T0353245

KATE GRENVILLE

Kate Grenville's novels include *The Secret River* (shortlisted for the Man Booker Prize and winner of the Commonwealth Writers' Prize and the NSW Premier's Literary Award), *The Idea of Perfection* (winner of the Orange Prize) and *Lilian's Story* (winner of the Australian/Vogel Prize). Her novel *Dark Places* was nominated for the Man Booker Prize, was shortlisted for the Miles Franklin Literary Award and won the Victorian Premier's Award for Fiction. *The Secret River*, *The Lieutenant* and her most recent novel, *Sarah Thornhill*, together make up *The Colonial Trilogy*, novels which explore Australia's often-troubled past. *The Secret River* was adapted as a TV mini-series. Most recently Kate Grenville has written two works of non-fiction, *One Life: My Mother's Story* and *The Case Against Fragrance*.

ANDREW BOVELL

Andrew was awarded the prestigious Patrick White Fellowship by the Sydney Theatre Company in 2017, and an Honorary Doctorate of Letters by Flinders University in 2018. His work has been seen in London at the Hampstead Theatre, the Almeida, the Lyric Hammersmith, and on the West End at the Duke of York's Theatre.

His most recent work for the stage, *El Jardín*, premiered at Teatro Principal in Zaragoza and was the result of a collaboration with Madrid Numero Zero collective.

Things I Know to Be True premiered in Adelaide in May 2016 in a co-production between the State Theatre Company and the UK's Frantic Assembly. The production opened in London at the Lyric Hammersmith in September before touring the UK. It returned to the Lyric Hammersmith and an extensive UK tour in 2017/2018. A new production opened at Belvoir St Theatre in 2019. The American premiere opened in March 2019 at the Milwaukee Rep Theatre and toured to Tucson and Phoenix. It opened in Madrid in November 2019.

The Secret River premiered at the Roslyn Packer Theatre in the 2013 Sydney Festival. The acclaimed STC production won six Helpmann Awards including Best Play, as well as Best New Work at the Sydney Theatre Awards, the Awgie Award for stage writing, the David Williamson Prize and the NSW Premier's Literary Award for Community Relations. It returned to the Ros Packer Theatre in Feb 2016 before touring to Brisbane and Melbourne. It was revived again for the 2017 Adelaide Festival of the Arts where it was performed in the Anstey Quarry. It opened at the Edinburgh International Festival and the National Theatre in London in 2019.

When the Rain Stops Falling premiered at the 2008 Adelaide Festival, produced by Brink Productions, before touring nationally and going on to win numerous awards. The play has been produced in London at the Almeida Theatre (2009) and in New York at The Lincoln Centre (2010), where it won five Lucille Lortell Awards and was named best new play of the year by *Time* Magazine. The play premiered in Spain in 2015 as *Cuando Deje De Llover* where it won four prestigious Max Awards. It opened in Rome at the Teatro Argentine in February 2019, and returned to an Italian tour in 2020.

Earlier works for the stage include *Fever*, *Holy Day*, *Who's Afraid of the Working Class?*, *Speaking in Tongues*, *Scenes from a Separation*, *Shades of Blue*, *Ship of Fools*, *After Dinner*, *The Ballad of Lois Ryan* and *State of Defense*. The Sydney Theatre Company revived his first play, *After Dinner*, for a sell-out season at the Wharf Theatre in Sydney in 2015, and the State Theatre Company produced the play in 2018.

For film he has adapted the American novel *Stoner* by John Williams. Other films include the French-language *In the Shadow of Iris*, directed by Jalil Lespert (2017). *A Most Wanted Man* is an adaptation of the John le Carré novel, directed by Anton Corbijn and staring Phillip Seymour Hoffman, Robyn Wright and Willem Defoe. The film premiered at the 2014 Sundance Film Festival. Other films include *Edge of Darkness*, which starred Mel Gibson, *Blessed* (winner of Best Screenplay at the San Sebastian Film Festival), *The Book of Revelation*, *Head On*, *Strictly Ballroom*, and the multi-award winning *Lantana*, which was based on his play *Speaking in Tongues*.

In September 2018, Andrew delivered the Wal Cherry Lecture at Flinders University. In 2015, he delivered the BAFTA and BFI International Screenwriting Lecture – the first Australian to be invited to do so. He delivered the landmark 2013 keynote address at the National Play Festival in Sydney and the 2011 Foxtel Address on Screenwriting. Andrew has served on the international jury for Sydney Film Festival, is a current board member of Playwriting Australia, and has served on the Literature Board of the Australia Council, and the boards of the Adelaide Film Festival and Australian Writers' Guild. He is a recipient of the Australian Centenary Medal for his services to the Arts and Society. He has served as a screenwriting consultant and mentor in Australia and Europe and has delivered numerous masterclasses on screenwriting and playwriting both in Australia and abroad.

THE SECRET RIVER

by

Kate Grenville

adapted for the stage by

Andrew Bovell

NICK HERN BOOKS

London

www.nickhernbooks.co.uk

A Nick Hern Book

This adaptation of *The Secret River* first published as a paperback original in Great Britain in 2019 by Nick Hern Books Limited, The Glasshouse, 49a Goldhawk Road, London W12 8QP, by arrangement with Currency Press Pty Ltd, PO Box 2287, Strawberry Hills, NSW 2012, Australia, www.currency.com.au

Adapted from *The Secret River* by Kate Grenville, copyright © Kate Grenville 2005
First published by The Text Publishing Company, Australia, 2005
Stage play adaptation copyright © Andrew Bovell, 2013
Foreword copyright © 2013 Henry Reynolds
Introduction copyright © 2013 Andrew Bovell

Cover photograph by Tom Huntley / Newspix

Andew Bovell has asserted his right to be identified as the author of this adaptation

Typeset by Nick Hern Books, London
Printed and bound in Great Britain by Mimeo Ltd, Huntingdon, Cambridgeshire PE29 6XX

A CIP catalogue record for this book is available from the British Library

ISBN   978 1 84842 870 6

CAUTION   All rights whatsoever in this play are strictly reserved. Requests to reproduce the text in whole or in part should be addressed to the publisher.

Performing Rights   All applications for public performance should be addressed to HLA, PO Box 1536, Strawberry Hills, NSW, 2012, *tel* +61 2 9549 3000, *fax* +61 2 9310 4113, *email* hla@hlamgt.com.au

No performance of any kind may be given unless a licence has been obtained. Applications should be made before rehearsals begin. Publication of this play does not necessarily indicate its availability for performance.

Woodland
CARBON
www.woodlandcarbon.co.uk
NICK HERN BOOKS
Printed on Carbon Captured paper

Contents

Foreword *by Henry Reynolds*   vii

Introduction *by Andrew Bovell*   xiii

Production Details   xx

Acknowledgements   xxiv

The Secret River   1

    Prologue   5

    Act One   13

    Act Two   58

    Epilogue   101

Music   104

Foreword
Henry Reynolds

It was while walking over Sydney Harbour Bridge that Kate Grenville experienced the epiphany which led to the writing of her novel *The Secret River*. She took part in the great procession for reconciliation on Sunday, 28 May 2000. She caught the eye of a young Aboriginal woman who was watching the marchers file past. They exchanged smiles. At the time Kate was thinking about her ancestor, Solomon Wiseman, about whom there was a living tradition of oral history and which took her family's historical memory back to the first generation of European settlement. She wondered if Wiseman had ever known the ancestors of the Aboriginal woman. What seemed even more significant was that the fleeting encounter took place directly above the likely location of Wiseman's disembarkation from the convict transport in 1806.

Family history and the national desire for reconciliation met and merged. Both propelled Grenville into a period of intense research into the history of early New South Wales. On the one hand she came to appreciate the profound importance of the indigenous history which continued to run beside the well-known stories of white pioneers. An even more profound realisation was that when Solomon Wiseman 'took up land' on the Hawkesbury River, he had actually taken land from the traditional owners; that the family's early opulence was based on expropriation. And that it was most likely effected at some time by indiscriminate violence perpetrated either by Wiseman himself or by friends and associates. Grenville's experience mirrored that of Judith Wright a generation earlier. Wright had set out to write an account of her pioneering ancestors. As she proceeded she discovered how family members had moved north from New England and been involved in the violent settlement in central Queensland. Both poet and novelist were profoundly shaken by the unexpected turn in family history and their discovery of the long-hidden history of violence.

It took Grenville five years of research and twenty drafts before the book was published. It was dedicated to 'the Aboriginal people of Australia: present, past and future'. Controversy swirled around her soon after it was launched in 2005: debate about fiction and history, intense at the time, distracted attention from the real significance of the work. But it did not deter readers. The book was reprinted ten times in two years. It sold over 100,000 copies and was subsequently translated into twenty languages. It won prizes both in Australia and overseas. Clearly *The Secret River* was a book for the times. Readers were avid for its message.

The same appears to be the case with Andrew Bovell's stage play adapted from the novel. It was the first work commissioned by Andrew Upton and Cate Blanchett for the Sydney Theatre Company in 2006, soon after the initial publication. The time lag between novel and play has not diminished the power of the story. Capacity audiences in Sydney, Canberra and Perth in March 2013 gave the players standing ovations – sometimes after moments of stunned silence. Many people cried. Few were untouched. *The West Australian* observed how the river ran deep for the Perth audiences. Critics in Sydney declared that a classic of Australian theatre had appeared.

The success of the play can be credited to the actors, the production team, and especially to the celebrated director Neil Armfield. But underpinning all their creative endeavour was Bovell's brilliant adaptation of the novel. His work was certainly facilitated by Grenville's willingness to stay at arm's length, requesting only that the script writing result in a good play. But even with the novelist's detached cooperation the task was challenging.

Novels and plays share some things in common. They characteristically adopt a narrative structure and unfold stories through time. At their best they create characters whose personalities and passions drive the action forward. But the differences between the two genres are greater than the things they share. A novelist can use an abundance of words. Grenville unfolds her story over 330 pages in well over 100,000 words. She is able to provide almost endless detail about people and places and material objects. She can reveal her characters with a slow accretion of knowledge and insight in the way we get to know people in real life. So like anyone adapting a novel for the stage Bovell had to whittle the story down in time and place while maintaining the cast of principal characters and elucidating the most significant themes. He had to abridge rather than adapt, preserving the essence of the novel and those events and the dialogue which made it significant in the first place.

The 330-page novel was pared down in both time and space. The first two sections, set in London and Sydney, are jettisoned while providing Bovell with a past allowing retrospective allusions that enrich the dialogue and give added depth to the main European characters, William and Sal Thornhill. All the events take place on the banks of the Hawkesbury River over a seven-month period in 1813 and 1814. The central focus is on a forty-hectare patch of cleared land where Thornhill has decided to start farming with his wife and two boys. At one level it is a classic story of pioneering, of the hardships and vicissitudes experienced by aspiring smallholders all over the continent throughout the nineteenth century.

But the audience immediately knows that this is a much more complicated story. As the play begins an Aboriginal extended family of five adults and two boys sit around a campfire. An Aboriginal narrator sets the scene speaking in English, but the group around the fire use Dharug, the local language. There are no surtitles. The audience does not know what they are saying. This was a bold decision by Bovell, Armfield and his associate director, choreographer Stephen Page. It made sense intellectually to have the Dharug speaking the language of the place. It emphasised the difficulty they had in communicating with the settlers and in turn their difficulty in trying to make themselves understood. In this way the audience is drawn directly into one of the great problems of the actual historical situation. But it is a tribute to the Aboriginal cast that they fluently use, what to them is a foreign language, with such ease of expression that for much of the time the gist of what is being said is grasped by members of the audience.

They are able to intuitively appreciate the way the Dharug experienced the tension and the misunderstanding inherent in the situation. But the full understanding is provided by the six settlers who Bovell chose from Grenville's larger cast, who come and go on stage, and above all by Will and Sal Thornhill and their two sons who build their hut and plant their corn on the Dharug's yam ground. At the very centre of the drama is the fact that the two groups both claim and endeavour to harvest the same plot of land. The flat, fertile land which produced the yams was also the best land for growing corn. The deep resonance of the situation becomes apparent to the audience. Bovell astutely uses Thornhill as a colonial everyman to articulate the ideas about land which were repeated endlessly all over the continent and justified the endless expropriation. The audience knows, as Thornhill cannot, that his situation will be recapitulated for generations to come under many different skies.

The central problem is articulated when we first meet the Thornhills. Will declares he wants a piece of land he could put his name on. 'And why not?', he asks. 'It's there for the taking.' To which his wife replies: 'But how can it be? What about those that are there?' He responds: 'They're not like us. They keep moving. They don't dig down into a place. They just move across it. Put up a decent fence and they'll get the idea.' In conversation with his son, Will observes:

A tent is all very well, lad, but what marks a man's claim is a square of dug-over dirt and something growing that had not been there before. This way, by the time the corn's sticking up out of the ground, any bugger passing in a boat will know this patch is taken. Good as raising a flag.

He tries to explain the situation to the traditional owners, declaring:

This is mine now. That's a 'T', Thornhill's place. You got all the rest. You got the whole blessed rest of it, mate, and welcome to it. But not this bit. This is mine.

Bovell's dialogue allows us to understand the settlers' lust for land. They had been cast out from a society where land ownership was the key determinant of status. It was unthinkable that they could ever have become proprietors in Britain. And it was the apparent ease of acquisition which gave promise of a better life at the antipodes and what reconciled them to their exile. It was what converted unwilling exiles into committed colonists.

Both Bovell and Armfield gave the production an added
dimension by offering intimations of what might have been a
more conciliatory outcome of the encounter. The younger of the
Thornhill boys plays happily with his Dharug counterparts.
Several of the settlers have achieved a sort of accommodation.
The elderly widow, Mrs Herring, understands the importance of
sharing. Thomas Blackwood, to the disgust of his fellow settlers,
has taken a Dharug wife, Dulla Dyin, and has a mixed-descent
child. Dulla Dyin uses traditional medicine to save pregnant Sal
Thornhill's life. Bovell and Armfield emphasise the common
humanity of Dhurag and European in the set with the two families
serially sharing the same camp fire.

But the tension inherent in the situation eventually engulfs
everyone. It was an outcome that was to be repeated again and
again as the settlers swept into new districts for the next hundred
years. Armfield skilfully controls the increasing tension. Anyone
who had read Grenville's book knew what was going to happen.
The settlers gather for what becomes a massacre of men, women
and children. Thornhill provides the boat for the venture and
takes part in the killing. Armfield eschews a scene of graphic
brutality but is able to allude to the horror of it all, leaving the
audience stunned.

There is then a double tragedy which gives the play greater depth.
All chance of accommodation is lost and Thornhill, who is
sympathetically portrayed, finally joins the brutal men of blood,
personified by the egregious Smasher Sullivan. But it all begs the
question of whether a more peaceful outcome was ever possible.
The historical record suggests otherwise. The die was cast even
before Thornhill was transported. The decision of the British
Government to declare New South Wales *terra nullius* and refuse
to recognise any indigenous land tenure was the over-mastering
decision. The Hawkesbury settlers had every reason to assume the
land in the valley was vacant Crown land. The Dharug therefore
had nothing to negotiate with. There was no need for the settlers
to learn their language or to understand their method of land use
or form of government. But the British Government was even
more directly culpable. With settlement extending up the
Hawkesbury, the Governor and his officials realised they could
not possibly police the frontier. They were forced to acquiesce in
settler violence. Bovell uses the actual words of a proclamation

issued by Governor Macquarie and published in the *Sydney Gazette* which are read to the settlers by Loveday – the one literate individual among them. The proclamation declared that if the Aborigines refused to leave land claimed by a settler they were to be 'driven away by force of arms by the settlers themselves'. Loveday sums it all up with the observation: 'Put plain, we may now shoot the buggers whenever we damn well please.'

The most portentous moment in the play is when Thornhill returns from Sydney with a gun. He had never owned one before and doesn't know how to use it. But during the massacre he shoots Yalamundi, the senior man of the band whose land he had assumed was his own, putting the expropriation beyond doubt.

Bovell's great achievement is to employ a small cast in a single location over a brief moment of time to unfold one of the archetypal stories of Australian settlement. It is for that reason that the play may well become one of the classics of the Australian stage.

May 2013

Henry Reynolds is an historian who works in Tasmania; his book Forgotten War *was published by NewSouth Books in 2013*.

Introduction
Andrew Bovell

The arc of Kate Grenville's novel is epic. It tells the story of
William Thornhill, born into brutal poverty on the south side of
London in the late-eighteenth century, his place in the world
already fixed by the rigidity of the English class system. In 1806
he is sentenced to hang for the theft of a length of Brazil wood.
Through the desperate efforts of his wife, Sal, his sentence is
commuted to transportation to the Colony of New South Wales. In
this new land he sees an opportunity to be something more than he
could ever have been in the country that shunned him. He sees 'a
blank page on which a man might write a new life'. He falls in
love with a patch of land on the Hawkesbury River and dares to
dream that one day it might be his. After earning his freedom he
takes Sal and their children from Sydney Cove to the Hawkesbury
to 'take up' a hundred acres of land, only to discover that the land
is not his to take. It is owned and occupied by the Dharug people.
As Thornhill's attachment to this place and his dream of a better
life deepens he is driven to make a choice that will haunt him for
the rest of his life.

Sometimes the best approach to adapting a novel is simply to get
out of the way. This proved to be the case with *The Secret River*.
The novel is much loved, widely read and studied. It has become
a classic of Australian literature. My task was simply to allow
the story to unfold in a different form. It took me some time to
realise this. Initially, I favoured a more lateral approach to the
adaptation. I wanted to project the events of the novel forward in
time and place the character of Dick Thornhill at the centre of
the play.

Dick is the second-born son of William and Sal. Arriving on the
Hawkesbury he is immediately captivated by the landscape and
intrigued by the people who inhabit it. With a child's curiosity
and open heart he finds a place alongside the Dharug and they,
perhaps recognising his good intentions, are at ease with his

presence among them. Unlike his older brother, Willie, he has no fear of the Dharug and seems to recognise that they understand how to live and survive in this place. He learns from them and tries to impart this knowledge to his father. William Thornhill's failure to learn the lesson his son tries to teach him is central to the book's tragedy.

When Dick discovers that his father has played an instrumental role in the massacre of the very people he has befriended, he leaves his family and goes to live with and care for Thomas Blackwood, who has been blinded in the course of the settler's violent attack on the Dharug.

One of the most haunting images of the book is contained in the epilogue. Thornhill, now a prosperous and established settler on the Hawkesbury, sits on the veranda of his grand house built on a hill and watches his estranged son passing on the river below onboard his skiff. He lives in hope that one day Dick will look up and see him. But Dick never does. He has made his choice and keeps his eyes steadfastly ahead, refusing to acknowledge his father and all that he has built.

Perhaps I was drawn to Dick because I'd like to think that if I found myself in those circumstances I would share his moral courage and turn my back on my own father, if I had to. I would hope that I too would refuse the prosperity gained from the act of violence and dispossession that the novel describes. I suspect, though, that like many at the time, I would have justified it as a necessary consequence of establishing a new country and found a way to live with it by not speaking of it. I would have chosen silence as so many generations of white Australians did.

It was here that I wanted to begin the play; on the moment of Thornhill watching his estranged son passing on the river. I created an imagined future for Dick. The novel reveals that Tom Blackwood had an Aboriginal 'wife' and that they had a child together. The gender of this child is not specified but I imagined that if she was a girl, that once grown, she and Dick might have 'married' and eventually had children of their own. So whilst William Thornhill and his descendants prospered on the banks of the Hawkesbury and became an established family of the district, another mob of Thornhills lived a very different life upriver, like a shadow of their prosperous cousins.

I mapped out a life for these two branches of the same family over several generations until I came to their contemporary incarnations. One family was white, the other black. I wondered whether they would be aware of their shared past and how the act of violence which set them on their separate paths would be carried through each generation, and whether reconciliation was ever possible between them. I imagined the story of Australia being revealed through the very different stories of these two families who shared a common ancestor and a dark secret. Importantly, in my mind was the idea that through the generations of Dick Thornhill's descendents, Aboriginal identity had not only survived but had strengthened.

My collaborators, Neil Armfield and Stephen Page, and the Artistic Directors of the Sydney Theatre Company, Andrew Upton and Cate Blanchett, heard me out but encouraged me to return to the book. They were right to do so. Perhaps by inventing this other story I was simply delaying the inevitable confrontation with the material at hand. Besides, Kate Grenville answered my curiosity about what happened to Dick Thornhill in her sequel to the novel, *Sarah Thornhill*. However, reaching beyond the source material into an imagined future was an important part of the process for me. I was trying to come to terms with the legacy of the violence depicted in the novel. I wanted to understand how this conflict is still being played out today.

When a connection is drawn so clearly between then and now, history starts to seem very close. I think this is one of the novel's great achievements. In William Thornhill, Kate Grenville has created a figure modern audiences can recognise and empathise with. He is a loving husband and father, a man who wants to rise above the conditions into which he was born and secure a better future for those who will come after him. This aspiration seems to me to be quintessentially Australian, and Nathaniel Dean who played the role beautifully captured this sense of a common man.

Once Grenville has placed us so surely in Thornhill's shoes she leads us into moral peril, for we find ourselves identifying with the decisions he makes. We may not agree with them but we understand them. And so we come to understand that the violence of the past was not undertaken by evil men, by strangers to us, but by men and women not unlike ourselves. That's the shock of it.

Grenville wasn't writing about them. She was writing about us. Above all I wanted to retain that sense of shock.

A number of key decisions started to give shape to the work. We decided to use the device of a narrator. This allowed us to retain some of Grenville's poetic language. We gave the narrator the name Dhirrumbin, which is the Dharug name for the Hawkesbury River. In effect she is the river, a witness to history, present before, during and after the events of the play. She knows from the start how the story ends and it falls upon her to recount the tragedy of it. This quality of knowing gives Dhirrumbin a sense of prophetic sadness. Ursula Yovich, who played the role, seemed to innately understand this. It wasn't until I first heard her read the part that I thought it could work. She brought great dignity and presence to the telling. As well as performing the classic task of moving the narrative forward, Dhirrumbin stands apart from the action and is able to comment on it. Even more importantly, she is able to illuminate the interior worlds of the characters, particularly the Dharug, and hence act as a bridge to our understanding of their experience.

Building the Dharug presence in the play was fundamental to our approach, and became one of the key differences between the play and the novel. Grenville chose to keep the Dharug characters at a distance. They are seen only through Thornhill's and the other white characters' eyes, and their actions and motivations are explained through the white characters' comprehension and often misinterpretation of them. In part, Kate chose to do this for cultural reasons. She felt there was a line that, as a white writer, she couldn't cross and that it was not possible to empathise with the traditional Aboriginal characters.

We didn't have that choice. It's an obvious point to make, but in transforming words on a page into live action on a stage we rely on the work of actors. And we simply couldn't have silent black actors on stage being described from a distance. They needed a voice. They needed an attitude. They needed a point of view. They needed language.

We assumed that there wasn't one available to us. We thought that the languages spoken around the Hawkesbury had largely been lost. For a while it seemed like an insurmountable problem. And then Richard Green, an actor and Dharug man, joined the project.

We put the problem to him. He laughed and opened his mouth and spoke and sang in Dharug. It was, he argued passionately, a lie that the language didn't exist. If it had been lost it had now been refound, rebuilt and reclaimed. It was a living language. And no white academic was going to tell Richard that he had no language. He enlivened the rehearsal room with his presence and gave us the confidence to find the voices for the Dharug characters. He translated the language and made it fit the needs of the production, and he taught the ensemble how to speak it and sing it.

We began by giving the Dharug characters names in their own language; Whisker Harry in the book became Yalamundi in the play, Long Jack became Ngalamalum, Polly became Buryia, Meg became Gilyagan, and Blackwood's unnamed wife, Dulla Dyin, and so on. In this simple act of naming the characters the Dharug world began to live on stage.

The task of representing a traditional indigenous point of view in what is a white narrative about history is fraught with difficulty and cultural sensitivity. Even with the best intentions and thorough research and consultation, a number of assumptions are still made. I wrote a line for Garraway, one of the children. 'I hate snake', he says as his mother is preparing a meal in the same way as a contemporary child might say 'I hate broccoli'. Richard pointed out that there was no word for hate, as such. But even the idea that a child in a traditional indigenous context would express dislike for a food central to their diet is an assumption we can't really make.

This is perhaps the greatest challenge for white storytellers in this country – how do we make sense of what indigenous peoples thought and felt about the arrival of Europeans in this country? Even first-hand accounts from the time have been written down and interpreted by European writers. We can only be led by contemporary indigenous people who, with great generosity, show us the way back so that we may begin to reconcile with our past.

Perhaps the greatest departure we made from the novel was to begin on the Hawkesbury and therefore to lose the part of the story set in London. This section provides an insight into Thornhill's deep relationship with Sal and with the River Thames, and importantly it depicts the social and political conditions into which he was born and which shaped his character. It is full of rich detail about the place and the times and the man himself. And yet, from a dramatic point of view, it was simply backstory to the central narrative. The point of greatest conflict, which is the bread and butter of drama, was the moment when black and white came together. I wanted to bring an audience to it as quickly as possible. It was in this relationship that the greatest interest and drama lay.

The novel came alive for me on that first night in Sydney, when on a dark night, with Sal and the boys asleep in a crude shelter behind him, Thornhill comes face to face with a black man and he is terrified. 'Be off,' he says. And this man repeats back to him in imitation, 'Be off'. This tense exchange encapsulates the central dilemma of the novel. Two men face each other on a dark night and both want the other gone. It is interesting that Kate chose to open the novel with this moment in a prologue before she took us back in time to London and formally began the story. The moment not only presents the central dilemma of the novel, it encapsulates our historical dilemma – two peoples with a different understanding of the land and its ownership come face to face. The question was whose definition of ownership of land would prevail.

History has answered that question, but the novel and therefore the play suggest that a different outcome was possible. Thomas Blackwood, Thornhill's neighbour and the closest thing he had to a friend on the river, found a way to share the land. He understood the nature of reciprocity. It was a matter of give a little, take a little, and of knowing your place. Similarly, the old woman, Mrs Herring, found a way to live peaceably alongside the Dharug by looking away when she needed to. In contrast, Smasher Sullivan, the lime burner, met the indigenous presence with brutal and unreasoned violence. This contrast was played out to a lesser degree also between Thornhill's sons. Dick sought to learn from the Dharug whilst Willie was always urging his Dad to 'get the gun'.

Ironically the same argument was taking place amongst the Dharug. Ngalamalum, played by Trevor Jamieson, could see where the situation was heading and favoured a more aggressive response to the intruders. Whilst the old man, Yalamundi, played by Roy Gordon, counselled a wait-and-see approach, tragically believing that the whites would move on soon or if they didn't would see the sense of the Dharug's relationship to the land and emulate it.

Even Sal, at first terrified by the Dharug, soon came to terms with the situation and began an economic relationship with Buryia and Gilyagan through the trading of goods, and even came to regard them as friends. Thornhill could have taken Sal's lead. He could have learned the lesson Dick wanted to teach him. He could have followed the path of Thomas Blackwood. Instead he chose to align himself with Smasher and the other settlers and embark upon a murderous assault against the Dharug as they lay sleeping.

In one of the production's most powerful moments the nursery rhyme 'London Bridge', first sung by Sal to her sleeping sons early in the play, has by the end become a battle cry sung by the men as they march, guns firing, into the Dharug camp.

Thornhill's choice to participate in the massacre does not leave him unscarred. In the book he is a haunted figure in an ill-fitting gentleman's coat, watching the surrounding hills for signs of the Dharug's return. Perhaps he fears that they will return to claim their place, knowing that his own claim is tenuous. And yet, I think Grenville is hinting at something deeper. It's as though their absence from the landscape is like a psychic wound he and the generations that follow will carry.

In the play we leave Thornhill maniacally painting a fence on the back wall of the set to mark his land as his own and to keep those others out. And yet the fence starts to resemble prison bars and it's not entirely clear which side of the bars Thornhill is standing on. Whilst Ngalamalam, who survived the massacre, sits by the fire. 'This me... My place', he says.

June 2013

The Secret River was first produced by Sydney Theatre Company at the Roslyn Packer Theatre, Sydney, on 12 January 2013, the cast was as follows:

DHIRRUMBIN / DULLA DYIN	Ursula Yovich
WILLIAM THORNHILL	Nathaniel Dean
SAL THORNHILL	Anita Hegh
WILLIE THORNHILL	Lachlan Elliott & Callum McManis
DICK THORNHILL	Rory Potter & Tom Usher
YALAMUNDI	Roy Gordon
BURYIA	Ethel-Anne Gundy
NGALAMALUM	Trevor Jamieson
GILYAGAN / MURULI	Miranda Tapsell
WANGARRA / BRANYIMALA	Rhimi Johnson Page
NARRABI	James Slee
GARRAWAY / DULLA DYIN'S CHILD	Kamil Ellis & Bailey Doomadgee
THOMAS BLACKWOOD	Colin Moody
SMASHER SULLIVAN	Jeremy Sims
MRS HERRING	Judith McGrath
SAGITTY BIRTLES / SUCKLING / TURNKEY	Matthew Sunderland
LOVEDAY	Bruce Spence
DAN OLDFIELD	Daniel Henshall
MUSICIAN / COMPOSER	Iain Grandage

All other roles were played by the company

Director	Neil Armfield
Artistic Associate	Stephen Page
Set Designer	Stephen Curtis
Costume Designer	Tess Schofield
Lighting Designer	Mark Howett
Sound Designer	Steve Francis

This project was assisted by the Australian Government's Major Festivals Initiative, managed by the Australia Council, its arts funding and advisory body, in association with the Confederation of Australian International Arts Festivals, Perth International Arts Festival, Sydney Festival and the Centenary of Canberra.

The Secret River had its UK premiere as part of the Edinburgh International Festival at King's Theatre, Edinburgh, on 3 August 2019 (previews from 2 August). The production subsequently transferred to the Olivier auditorium of the National Theatre, London, on 22 August 2019. The cast was as follows:

SAL THORNHILL	Georgia Adamson
DAN OLDFIELD	Joshua Brennan
DICK THORNHILL	Toby Challenor
NGALAMALUM	Shaka Cook
WANGARRA / BRANYIMALA	Marcus Corowa
WILLIAM THORNHILL	Nathaniel Dean
MUSICIAN	Isaac Hayward
MRS HERRING	Melissa
JAFFER BURYIA	Elma Kris
DHIRRUMBIN / DULLA DJIN	Ningali Lawford-Wolf
NARABI	Dylan Miller
THOMAS BLACKWOOD	Colin Moody
GARRAWAY / DULLA DJIN'S CHILD	Jacob Narkle & Wesley Patten
WILLIE THORNHILL	Rory Potter
SMASHER SULLIVAN	Jeremy Sims
LOVEDAY	Bruce Spence
YALAMUNDI	Major 'Moogy' Sumner
SAGITTY BIRTLES / SUCKLING / TURNKEY	Matthew Sunderland
GILYAGAN / MURULI	Dubs Yunupingu

Director	Neil Armfield
Artistic Associate	Stephen Page
Set Designer	Stephen Curtis
Costume Designer	Tess Schofield
Lighting Designer	Mark Howett
Composer	Iain Grandage
Musical Director	Isaac Hayward

Sound Designer	Steve Francis
Tour Director	Geordie Brookman
Dramaturg	Matthew Whittet
Voice & Text Coach	Charmian Gradwell
Language Consultant	Richard Green
Additional Music	Trevor Jamieson
Fight Director	Scott Witt
Senior Producer	Ben White
Associate Producer	Zoe O'Flanagan
Company Manager	Sarah Stait
Touring Company Manager	Amelia Mullinar
Auntie-in-Residence	Auntie Glendra Stubbs
Production Manager	Kate Chapman
Stage Manager	Sarah Smith
Deputy Stage Manager	Todd Eichorn
Assistant Stage Manager	Jaymii Knierum
Assistant Stage Manager	Georgiane Deal
Pre-Tour Costume Coordinators	Catherine Mayne and Scott Fisher
Wig, Make Up and Wardrobe Supervisor	Lauren A. Proietti
Head Mechanist	Steve Mason
Production Electrician	Andrew Tompkins
FOH Sound Operator	David Bergman
Radio Mic Technician	Olivia Benson
Rehearsal Chaperone	Jai Greenaway

Acknowledgements

The theatre is a place to tell the important stories that matter to our culture and our times. But such stories can't be told without the dedication of many people. *The Secret River* was the first project Cate Blanchett and Andrew Upton initiated after taking up their roles as co-Artistic Directors at the STC. The production is a testament to their shared vision for the company. I'd like to thank them and their team at the STC. Among them Rachel Azzopardi who found money where it didn't exist and said yes much more often than she said no. Jo Dyer wrangled the core artistic team in the early days and ensured that we found ourselves in the same city, in the same room at the same time, in order to get the work done. Polly Rowe listened to our conversations and encouraged us to keep talking. Annie Eves-Bolland and John Colvin led a dedicated production team. Georgina Gilbert and her stage-management team were extraordinary in their care for the show as they carried it through three cities. Colm O'Callaghan managed the company on tour, and Kip Williams, the assistant director, took charge of it when it was on the road.

David Gonski and Orli Wargon and Simon and Catriona Mordant generously supported the development of the project. Lovers of the book and the theatre, they recognised that this was a story worth telling.

The parameters of the adaptation were set out during many hours of conversation between Neil Armfield, Stephen Page and myself as we wrestled with a way to approach it. Matt Whittet joined the conversation in the first workshop and stayed on board as a dramaturg. Richard Green's presence was vital as a language consultant and Dharug song man.

I am full of admiration for Neil Armfield. He is one of our great storytellers. Sometimes a playwright is left feeling that there was more in the text than a production has managed to find. The opposite is the case here. Neil found more than I had imagined possible. He led a brilliant design team: Stephen Curtis (set), Tess

Schofield (costume), Mark Howett (lights) and Steve Francis (sound). Iain Grandage's presence in the rehearsal room and on stage was a gift to the production. He was more than a composer. He was one of the key storytellers and his use of the actors in creating the music for the production was inspired.

I often fall in love with actors, even when they are grumpy and don't like what you have asked them to do. Even when they forget your lines and make up their own. I'm a little in awe of them. They are raw and tender. Brittle and tough. They have to be to do what is asked of them. There were twenty-one of them in this show. And I want to name each of them.

The seven boys: Bailey Doomadgee, Lachlan Elliott, Kamil Ellis, Rory Potter, Callum McManis, James Slee and Tom Usher. They took to the stage like ducks to water. Literally. Their water fight was a highlight of the show. But the fun bits were easy. These kids also did death, shame, guilt and fear night after night.

Thanks Matthew Sunderland for dying every night with a teacup in your hand and making it work. Ethel-Anne Gundy and Miranda Tapsell created two beautiful characters out of the little that was given to them on the page. Rhimi Johnson Page never flinched once as a whip cracked centimetres from his face. I saw Daniel Henshall take a heavy fall in rehearsal and be back on his feet in minutes ready to work again despite the pain he was in. Judith McGrath captured a woman who had seen it all before and yet still cared enough to speak against the wrong of what took place. Bruce Spence's fallen Loveday stood out in the show almost as much as his kangaroo. Colin Moody didn't agree with everything in the play. 'Fifteen minutes too long and not deep enough', he said. It hurt but he was probably right. But every night I saw him perform he gave everything that was asked of him in the role of Tom Blackwood. Jeremy Sims was terrifying as Smasher Sullivan. Not easy to play a man with such a damaged psyche night after night. Roy Gordon brought great dignity to Yalamundi. Trevor Jamieson's Ngalamalum 'NO… This me… My place' will stay with me forever. Anita Hegh's Sal standing in defiance against Thornhill 'Hit me if you want, Will. But it won't change nothing. We're going. With or without you' still raises the hairs on the back of my neck. And her final moment on stage, as she stands, stranded, bewildered and alone in a place she doesn't want to be, was so painful.

I watched Nat Dean build the character of William Thornhill from the very first time he read the part. He wrestled with it and made it his own. He got all the goodness in the man, his love for his sons and his wife and place he wanted to call his own. But he got his ambition, his ruthlessness and his shame as well. A critic described his work in the play as a career-defining moment. I agree.

The role of narrator can be thankless. Ursula Yovich was on stage throughout the whole show holding the story in her powerful hands. I saw her break down several times in rehearsal. The role required a great deal from her. She didn't want to take it on. As an actor she wants to take on roles that go beyond her aboriginality. She has laid down a challenge to our industry to see beyond colour in casting. It's time we listened to her.

The final thanks goes to our author, Kate Grenville. On opening night we made her take a bow. She didn't want to do it. She was reluctant to take the moment. She tried to give it to me. To Neil. To the cast. But the moment was hers.

Kate dedicated her novel to the Aboriginal people of Australia: past, present and future. This play is written in the same spirit.

A.B.

THE SECRET RIVER

Kate Grenville

adapted for the stage by

Andrew Bovell

'Such a small boat, such a vast sea.'

Kate Grenville

4

Characters

DHIRRUMBIN, *the narrator*
WILLIAM THORNHILL, *an emancipist settler*
SAL THORNHILL, *his wife*
WILLIE THORNHILL, *his eldest son*
DICK THORNHILL, *his youngest son*
YALAMUNDI, *a Dharug elder man*
BURYIA, *a Dharug elder woman*
NGALAMALUM, *a Dharug man*
GILYAGAN, *a Dharug woman*
WANGARRA, *a younger Dharug man*
NARRABI, *a Dharug boy*
GARRAWAY, *a Dharug boy*
THOMAS BLACKWOOD, *a settler on the Hawkesbury River*
SMASHER SULLIVAN, *a settler*
MRS HERRING, *a settler*
SAGITTY BIRTLES, *a settler*
LOVEDAY, *a settler*
DAN OLDFIELD, *a convict*

CAPTAIN SUCKLING, BRANIYAMALA, DULLA DYIN, DULLA DYIN'S CHILD, MURULI, NEWGATE TURNKEY, CONVICTS *and the* DHARUG PEOPLE *at Darkey Creek are played by members of the cast.*

Dogs and kangaroos are also played by the cast.

Setting

The play is set on the Hawkesbury River between September 1813 and April 1814. The Dharug people who lived there at this time knew the river as Dhirrumbim.

Prologue

The River Flat.

Let us begin with the sound of water as it laps against the riverbank and of birds rising and of the wind gathering in the tops of the trees.

A family is gathered around a smouldering fire. YALAMUNDI, *the old man, and* BURYIA, *his wife –* NGALAMALUM *and* WANGARRA, GILYAGAN *and her sons,* NARRABI *and* GARRAWAY.

YALAMUNDI *is silent as he stares over the water as the others talk about the day to come.* BURYIA *is telling everyone what they should do and when they should do it. Nobody is listening much.*

BURYIA. Wyabuininyah minga waddiwadi yira guyun guwinga-da. Durunung biall barrawu, maana duruwan waru-ni maana. [*You lot, bring all the sticks and gather all those fruits. Bring them over here ready for cooking.*]

The boys are playing.

NARRABI. Ni durumin. [*Look at the girl.*]

GARRAWAY. Murray dyinmang. [*You're a bigger girl.*]

NARRABI. Guwuwi wawa. [*Come on, come at me.*]

NGALAMALUM. Gugugu wangarra. [*Stop it, boys.*]

GILYAGAN. Gugugu garranarbillie. [*Stop laughing around.*]

The boys get on with their job.

NARRABI. Wugal wadi. [*One stick.*]

GARRAWAY. Wadi wadi. [*Sticks.*]

NARRABI. Gugugu murray nin. [*Stop getting all the big ones.*]

GARRAWAY. Ngai Biji ngyinu. [*I'm better than you.*]

NARRABI. Ngai bugi bugi. [*I'll hit you with my stick.*]

BURYIA. Yan wungarra, yan wammalalibyila. [*You two, stop mucking about. Go on, go swimming together.*]

This only makes them laugh all the more. She waves them away, stern but already forgiving them.

GARRAWAY. Dienamillie? [*Wanna play?*]

NARRABI. Budyari / Yuin. [*Yes.*]

GARRAWAY (*calling after him*). Narrabi, Narrabi.

As they run off:

NGALAMALUM. Mudang wangarra. [*They're strong boys.*]

WANGARRA. Yuin mulla ingarang guni gabaras. [*Yes man, little shitheads.*]

Without warning or fanfare, YALAMUNDI *breaks into song – a mourning song. The others fall silent.* NGALAMALUM *and* WANGARRA *take up clapsticks and accompany him.*

As a figure emerges from the river, as if called by the song – DHIRRUMBIN, *our narrator.*

YALAMUND (*singing*).
    Nura-Da Nura-Da Nura-Da Nura-Da Nura-Da [*Country*]
    Nura-Da Nura-Da Nura-Da Nura-Da Nura-Da
    Guwuwi Guwuwi Nura-Da Nura-Da Nura-Da Nura-Da
        Nura-Da [*Calling out to country*]

DHIRRUMBIN (*as the song ends*). He saw the smoke from the nearby ridge. He knew what it meant. Someone was coming. They'd heard the stories passed down the river. Of strangers. And trouble. They'd seen the boats passing. This way and back. This way and back. And the old man, Yalamundi, felt the pain in his chest. Because he knew something was about to change. And he didn't know how to stop it. He wanted to. He wanted time to stand still.

While away from here, some thirty miles down the coast, another man sees a chance to be something more than what he is and a woman waits as she watches over her kids and sings a song from some faraway place.

* * *

Sydney Cove, the Thornhills' Hut.

SAL THORNHILL *sits by the light of a lamp. Her sons,* WILLIE *and* DICK, *have fallen asleep at her side.*

SAL (*singing softly*).
    London Bridge is falling down,
    Falling down, falling down,
    London Bridge is falling down,
    My fair lady.

    Who has stole my watch and chain,
    Watch and chain, watch and chain,
    Who has stole my watch and chain,
    My fair lady.

    Off to prison you must go,
    You must go, you must go.
    Off to prison you must go,
    My fair lady.

WILLIAM THORNHILL *enters.*

They wanted to wait up… Couldn't keep their eyes open in the end.

THORNHILL *looks upon his sons. He cares more for them than he has the words to say. He lifts* DICK *and lays him in the bed, and then* WILLIE, *as* SAL *covers them with a blanket.*

Well?

He takes a piece of paper from his pocket and hands it to her. She carefully unfolds it in the light of the lamp.

THORNHILL. What's it say?

SAL. Give a woman a chance.

She gathers herself. The words aren't easy.

(*Reading.*) 'By virtue of such Power and Authority so vested in me, I, Major General Lachlan Macquarie, Governor in Chief of His Majesty, George the Third's said Territory of New South Wales and its… something something… taking into consideration the good conduct of William Thornhill, who arrived on board *The Alexander*, in the charge of Captain James

Suckling in the Year One Thousand Eight Hundred and Six under Sentence of Transportation for Life, do grant the aforesaid... Absolute Pardon.'

A moment... a tear nearly shed.

THORNHILL. Don't.

SAL. Why not?

THORNHILL. Because you'll start me off.

SAL. You're free, William Thornhill... We can go home.

She folds the official paper into a piece of calico and places it into a box that contains their savings and other precious things.

What's he like... our Governor?

THORNHILL. He's a Scot. Could hardly make sense of a word he said. Liked the sound of my name coming out of his mouth, though. Last time a man of that station said my name it was to condemn me to hang.

SAL. That was a lifetime ago.

THORNHILL. Four years, Sal.

She takes a broken piece of tile from the box and kisses it before replacing it.

How much have we got?

SAL. Thirty-three pound. Not bad given what we came with.

THORNHILL. It's not enough though, is it? Not to take us back.

She is silent. She knows it's the truth.

We'll get it.

SAL. I know.

THORNHILL. A man named Walsh in Cockle Bay makes a decent one-man skiff. New oars can wait.

SAL. It's small though, Will. A boat like that, you can't work much beyond Sydney Cove. It's a slow way to get on.

THORNHILL. It's a living. And it would be ours.

SAL. Blackwood is selling *The Queen*.

THORNHILL. For a hundred and sixty pounds.

SAL. He'll take less. For you. What is she?

THORNHILL. Nineteen feet.

SAL. That's a boat made for a father and his sons.

THORNHILL. What are you saying?

SAL. We'll borrow the rest.

THORNHILL. Oh, yeah!

SAL. I've done the sums. With your reputation for work you'll get the loan and pay it back with interest. And with Blackwood retiring, you'll take over the Hawkesbury run. You know that's what he wants.

THORNHILL. He hasn't said it.

SAL. Well, he doesn't, does he? A man like Blackwood doesn't say much about much. But you've been his right-hand man. Stands to reason he'd want you to take over.

THORNHILL *is silent*.

If we don't take the chance these boys will be men before they breathe English air again. Think of it, Will. Home! Imagine that! And to go back as people with something in our pockets!

Beat.

What?

THORNHILL. I didn't say nothing.

SAL. No. But you're thinking it… You got something on your mind, you best be out with it.

THORNHILL. There's a piece of land I seen up there. Had my eye on it this past year.

SAL. Land?

THORNHILL. One hundred acres. About. With a flat spread by the water, not easy to find. And a rise behind with a handsome view.

SAL. A year you've been thinking this without telling me.

THORNHILL. And if I had what would've you said?

SAL. I'd 'ave told you to forget it.

THORNHILL. And you wonder why a man keeps things to himself… Get on faster with a crop to sell.

SAL. You a farmer!

THORNHILL. We should get it before some other bugger does.

SAL. Get it! What do you mean, get it?

THORNHILL. Blackwood says you just need to plant your backside somewhere and leave it there long enough and it's yours.

SAL. You're a fool if you think something comes that cheap.

THORNHILL. There's others done it. Grabbed a piece. Put in a crop to say it's theirs. Even given it their name.

SAL. A piece of land with your name on it! Is that what you're after?

THORNHILL. A different life is what I'm after.

Beat.

SAL. The only thing you know about a turnip is how to eat it.

THORNHILL. I'll learn.

SAL. You're a river man, Will. You've got river water for blood. You can trace the course of the Thames on the back of your hand. Every twist and turn. You know it like you know me. What do you know about planting and growing? The idea of it! No! We're doing well enough the way things are. You taking over the Hawkesbury run, couple of years we'll have enough to go back. Get a house in the Borough. On Swan Lane. Couple of wherries for you and the boys. An armchair by the fire for each of us. We've talked about it and now you're carrying on as if we never did. For a piece of land with your name on it!

THORNHILL. And why not? If it's there for the taking.

SAL. But how can it be? What about those that are there?

THORNHILL. That's all been done.

SAL. What's been done?

Beat.

What's been done, Will?

He is silent.

So the stories are true about what goes on up there?

THORNHILL. Only stories I hear are the ones told by men without the guts to go beyond Parramatta. You might see the smoke from a fire on a ridge now and then. But in all my trips up there, Sal, I can tell you I haven't seen a handful and only then in the distance.

SAL. You might not see them but they see you.

THORNHILL. Then let them... Let them see me. I'll tell them my name is William Thornhill.

SAL. I'm sure they'll be impressed. They'll say good day, Mr Thornhill, and then they'll stick you with their spear.

THORNHILL. They're not like us. They keep moving. They don't dig down into a place. They just move across it. Put up a decent fence and they'll get the idea.

SAL. And what about snakes?

THORNHILL. We've got snakes here.

SAL. But we've got a surgeon of sorts to put it right and a parson to say a prayer over a dead body. Christ, Will! Have you thought about that? The children. Hard enough to keep them alive here.

THORNHILL. Boys are old enough now. Willie will work on the boat with me. Dick can look after the crop and some hogs.

SAL. You've thought this through, haven't you?

WILLIE *raises his head from the blankets.*

THORNHILL. Hey, lad.

WILLIE. Ya free now, Da?

THORNHILL. As a bird, son. Got a piece of paper to say it too. I'll show you in the morning. Now back to sleep with you.

WILLIE *lies back down. A moment…*

It's a chance, pet. That's all.

She is silent and he sees in her face the door open and the crack of light beyond it.

Give it five years. Make our pack. Then we are on the first boat home.

SAL. Are you making me a promise?

THORNHILL. As God is my witness.

SAL. Five years then.

He goes to her and they kiss to seal the deal.

Just remember… you don't pick turnips off a tree.

THORNHILL. Christ, I love you.

SAL. Then you best do something about it.

THORNHILL. What if we wake them?

SAL. If we do we'll tell them we're dancing.

DHIRRUMBIN. They never tired of one another's touch. And any trouble between them could always be settled beneath the blanket.

They bought *The Queen* and not being fond of royalty renamed her *The Hope*. She set sail in the month of September in the year 1813.

As they rounded the North Head she met the ocean swell. There was a kind of thrill he felt every time *The Hope* was caught in the hand of the wind and the water. Such a small boat, such a vast sea.

He heard one of the boys cry out. In joy or fear. He could not tell. He kept his eyes forward and saw only a blank page on which a man might write a new life.

ACT ONE

Scene One

The River Flat and a Rough Camp.

As the shadows of dusk creep across the river and push up the length of the point, The Hope *remains stuck fast in the mud with* SAL *still on board among their bundles of provisions and belongings. The air is thick with sound. Birds are settling for the night and a chorus of insects fills her ears. She remains very still, as if to move would be to acknowledge that she had arrived.*

Suddenly WILLIE *and* DICK *burst from the bushes with* THORNHILL *a few paces behind.*

WILLIE. We got the tent up, Ma. And a nice fire to get you warm.

She is slow to move. THORNHILL *gives* DICK *a nudge to add something encouraging.*

DICK. And the kettle boiling for a drink of tea. And guess what?

SAL. What?

DICK. Ain't seen no savages.

THORNHILL. Yeah, alright, Dick. That's enough… You ready, pet?

SAL puts on a brave face and rises.

You make a path there for your ma… out of them branches.

SAL. I don't need no path made. I'm not Lady bloody Muck.

THORNHILL helps her down from the boat and she steps shin-deep into mud.

DICK. Aww, mud.

She silences the boys' laughter with a look.

THORNHILL. Don't laugh at your mother.

The boys make a path of broken branches before their mother, as THORNHILL *takes a box of provisions from the boat.*

They work their way up through the trees to a rough camp in a small clearing. A crude tent their only shelter, with a fire burning with the kettle half-fallen into the flames. All is quiet except for the sound of the birds settling for the night.

At last SAL *says something.*

SAL. Is this it then, Will?

THORNHILL. As snug as a flea in a dog's ear.

In the silence that follows, a rueful bird lets out its long cry of regret.

SAL *looks around for something she can recognise. Something that might tell her that someone could live here.*

SAL. We may as well be the only people in the world.

THORNHILL. There's others. Upriver. A bloke called Webb. Spider for short. And Loveday. A real gent before the booze got him. An old bird called Mrs Herring. And Blackwood, of course. Got himself a place up along the First Branch. Aways a way up.

SAL. I'll pop over for a cup of tea, shall I? Only take me a day to get there.

They try to laugh. A slither of a moon sits above the ridge.

THORNHILL. You see that moon? Same moon you see above London. And that river. Not too different to the Thames. Wider here. Narrower there. Smells better. And down there by the boat – that's where Christ Church would be, and our little track the Borough High Street, see it there?

He points at the cliffs above them.

Remember how steep it was like that, going up St Mary-at-Hill? Past Waterman's Hall and that? Ain't it just the same?

SAL. Still is. Still there where it always was. Only trouble is, we ain't.

THORNHILL. Five years won't be no time at all, Sal. You'll see.

DICK *takes her hand to reassure her. She looks down and sees the worry in his little face.*

SAL. Where's that cup of tea then?

The boys swing into action, stoking the fire with twigs as darkness begins to fall.

Least we won't be short of firewood.

They creep closer to the light of the fire as the night encircles them. The trees grow huge, hanging over them.

WILLIE. Might they be watching us, Da? Waiting like. The savages?

THORNHILL. Shut your trap, Willie. We ain't got nothing to worry about. There ain't nobody here but us.

The family stands in silence by the light of the fire as the black of the night grows all around them.

Scene Two

The Rise Above the Camp.

THORNHILL *stands on a platform of rock looking down to the camp and, beyond that, the river – his hundred acres laid out before him.*

DHIRRUMBIN. The next morning Sal rose early and swept a patch of dirt clean and called it 'the yard' as if that would make it a different place to all that surrounded it. It would become her place. Beyond that she went only for the call of nature, and did not dally.

THORNHILL (*as narrator*). Thornhill and the boys set to work cutting twenty saplings ready to make a start on their hut. With the day's work done he could no longer wait to climb the rise above the camp. He wanted to see the place all at once. And as he bashed his way through the bush, with each tree he touched he said this is my tree and with each rock he climbed he said this is my rock.

At last he came to a platform high above the camp and looked over his hundred acres. Thornhill's Point stretched out before him in the shape of a thumb. The river on each side. This is mine, he said. And he laughed at the thought of just how easy it was to own a piece of land. Is all a man had to do was stand on it.

(*As* THORNHILL.) I see you, Willy. By God, lad, I see you. And you too, Dick. Make sharp with that axe, my boys. My boys... One day this will be yours.

DHIRRUMBIN. And it shocked him... what he said. He had hardly let himself think it, let alone put words to the idea... that there might be something beyond five years. It frightened him... what it could mean. To Sal. But he couldn't deny it... Once spoken, the idea was hard to shift.

* * *

The Thornhills' Camp.

DICK (*singing*).
    Oranges and lemons,
    Say the bells of St Clement's.*

SAL *busies herself mixing a damper as she sings. The boys make the fire ready.*

SAL (*singing*).
    You owe me five farthings,
    Say the bells of St Martin's.

DICK (*singing*).
    When will you pay me?
    Say the bells of Old Bailey.

SAL (*singing*).
    When I grow rich...

THORNHILL *watches from the edge of the clearing, having returned from the ridge.*

THORNHILL. They're too old for nursery rhymes now, Sal.

* See page 104 for musical score.

SAL. Just a little bit of home. Can't hurt them.

THORNHILL *notices two lines marked in the trunk of a tree.*

THORNHILL. What's this?

WILLIE. We been here two days. Ma's counting them off.

THORNHILL *does not meet* SAL*'s eye… but nor does she meet his.*

THORNHILL. Tomorrow we'll start on that patch for the corn.

Scene Three

The River Flat.

Under the morning sun, THORNHILL *sweats as he strikes the earth with a pick, as* WILLIE *works behind him turning the dirt over with a spade, determined to keep pace with his da.*

DICK, *a dreamer, has wandered away a little dragging his hoe, distracted by something on the ground.*

THORNHILL. A tent is all very well, lad, but what marks a man's claim is a square of dug-over dirt and something growing that had not been there before. This way, by the time the corn's sticking up out of the ground, any bugger passing in a boat will know this patch is taken. Good as raising a flag.

DICK *picks up something from the ground… some kind of daisy plant with a fleshy white root. He looks around him on the ground trying to work something out.*

DICK. Look, Da! Some other bugger already dug it up.

THORNHILL *and* WILLIE *approach. It's true. There is a patch of freshly turned soil. A few daisies lay loose, their thick roots broken. He scuffs at one with his heel.*

THORNHILL. Just wild hogs or such. Moles. Something like that.

DICK. Moles? You reckon moles?

THORNHILL. A man did this it'd be dug in a square. This ain't no square. Just a lot of rooting around this place and that.

DICK. After these taters most like.

WILLIE. They ain't taters!

DICK. Sort of taters.

WILLIE *takes one and bites it. He spits it out.*

WILLIE. Don't taste like no tater.

THORNHILL *smacks it out of his hand.*

THORNHILL. What are you doing? Don't go biting things you don't know what they are! Now both of you, look sharp. Dirt's not going to get dug with us standing around talking about taters all day.

They return to work… breaking, digging, turning the soil, casting the daisy plants aside as they go.

DICK *is the first to look up sensing something… like he is being watched.*

Three men stand on the edge of the clearing. YALAMUNDI, NGALAMALUM *and* WANGARRA. *The two younger men hold spears.*

DICK. Da.

THORNHILL *and* WILLIE *look up and see them.*

As if he has been waiting for this moment, YALAMUNDI *steps forward. The moment is his.*

THORNHILL (*to the boys*). Don't move. Don't say a bloody word.

THORNHILL *swallows, his mouth suddenly feeling dry. He wipes his hands on the side of his britches and places them in his pockets… as if this would convince someone he wasn't too worried.*

Unable to bear it any longer, THORNHILL *approaches, speaking as he would to a pack of wary dogs.*

Don't spear me, there's a good man. I'd offer you a cup of tea, only we ain't got none.

YALAMUNDI *cuts across his words as if they were of no more importance than the rattle of wind in a tree. He gestures with a fluid hand down the river, up over the hills and does a flattening thing with his palm like smoothing a bedcover.*

YALAMUNDI. Diya ngalaium nura warrawarra. Ngaya Buruberongal. Ngalaium bembul. Murray murray nura. Durubin Ngayri mulbu. Ngyina ni diya nura. Ngan giyara? Wellamabami? [*This is our place. Our country. All around here. The river and beyond those ridges. We look after these places. Who are you? Where are you from?*]

THORNHILL (*trying to make a joke of it*). Old boy... bugger me, you are making no sense whatsoever!

Silence... as if he is waiting for more.

You ain't making no sense to me, mate. Not a blinking word. You might as well bloody bark.

WILLIE *barks like a dog...*

WILLIE. Ruff, ruff, ruff.

THORNHILL (*sharp as broken glass*). Shut your mouth!

WILLIE *steps back, shamed by the harshness of his father's words.*

YALAMUNDI *speaks again as he makes a chopping action with the side of his hand and points to the patch of dug-up daisies.*

YALAMUNDI. Biyall gama-da jillung midyini, ngyini guwuwi diem dane dharug. Ngyini maana bulla-bu, yan nin dane ngyinu. [*Don't dig up those yams. We come here for those. You take some, leave the rest for us.*]

NGALAMALUM. Nanu biyal manyuru. Nin yura ngaya ni. [*He doesn't understand. The same as the others.*]

YALAMUNDI. Ngmuun. [*Be quiet.*]

THORNHILL. Listen, old man... This is my place now. You got all the rest.

YALAMUNDI *does not look around to follow the sweep of*
THORNHILL's *arm. He knows what's there.*

WANGARRA. Mipidyadyimi? [*What's he saying?*]

NGALAMALUM. Nanu biningarri wingaru dah nanu nura. [*He
calls it his place.*]

SAL *appears, having heard the commotion from the camp. She
stifles a gasp and sums the situation up in a single glance.*

SAL. Willie, here… give them this piece of pork… look sharp.

WILLIE *runs to her and takes the wrapped piece of pork and
then takes it to his father.* THORNHILL *holds it out to them.*
YALAMUNDI *makes no gesture to take it.* THORNHILL *then
offers it to* NGALAMALUM. *The younger man accepts the
offer. He holds it in his hand.*

THORNHILL. It's food, mate. You eat it.

DICK. Don't think he follows you, Da.

THORNHILL *demonstrates eating.*

THORNHILL. Tastes good, mate…

YALAMUNDI. Byalla-da bada dah. [*Don't eat it.*]

THORNHILL. No, it's good food. Salt pork.

NGALAMALUM *puts the pork down on the dirt. He smells
his fingers, wrinkles his nose and wipes his hand on his thigh
as* WANGARRA *moves the pork further away with his foot.*

Then YALAMUNDI *makes a clear move and walks over to the
dug patch and seizes the spade.*

WILLIE. Oi! Give us that back, you thieving black!

SAL. Willie!

WILLIE *tries to grab it back. The old man wrenches himself
free. He shouts angrily… the same word over and over again.*

YALAMUNDI. Gu, gu, gu. Biyal. [*Stop, stop, stop. No.*]

WILLIE. Give it here. You thieving black.

THORNHILL. Leave it be, Willie.

THORNHILL *approaches and slaps* YALAMUNDI *hard in the shoulder. Once. Twice. Three times. And with each time…*

No! No! No! Not my sons.

The old man's face closes down into its creases of shadow. His hand reaches around and gets the curved wooden club from the string at his waist.

In an instant, NGALAMALUM *and* WANGARRA *have their spears raised and ready to throw.* SAL *runs forward and gathers the boys into a tight embrace to shield them.*

A tight-wound moment is held.

Then YALAMUNDI *gives a grunt of disgust and turns away, dropping the spade on the ground. He disappears into the forest.*

NGALAMALUM *runs forward until the point of the spear is at* THORNHILL*'s face.* SAL *screams. He pushes* THORNHILL *in the chest then slaps him three times hard in the shoulder, as* THORNHILL *had done to* YALAMUNDI.

NGALAMALUM. Biyal, biyal, biyal. [*Stop, stop, stop.*] Wurrawarra. [*Go away.*]

The meaning is clear. Even a dog would understand it. And then they go. The THORNHILLS *are silent. Stunned. Breathing.*

SAL. You said they'd gone.

THORNHILL. More than a dozen times I've been here. I swear. Camped at this very spot. Never seen a sign of them.

SAL. 'Cause you weren't looking, Will. You didn't want to see no sign.

DICK. They just don't want us to dig up their taters, Da, that's all.

THORNHILL. And what would you know about it?

Beat.

SAL. You two wait up at the camp.

The boys leave.

There's no shame in backing out of this.

THORNHILL. I'm not backing out of anything.

SAL. Go back to Sydney... make our pile from there. You still got the boat.

THORNHILL. You think a couple of skinny blackfellas waving a stick in my face worry me?

SAL. I'm frightened, Will. Not for myself... you know that. But for the boys.

THORNHILL. Nothing's going to happen to those boys.

Beat.

It's a misunderstanding, that's all. I'll work it out.

SAL. If you say so, Will.

She leaves.

THORNHILL *remains alone.*

Scene Three (a)

The Next Morning, First Light.

A heavy mist rises up from the river.

NGALAMALUM (*singing*).
Yilumay [*Spear*]
Yilumay [*Spear*]
Yilumay. [*Spear*.]

As spears descend...

THORNHILL *emerges from the tent. At first it seems as if a ring of new saplings have sprung up overnight until his stomach tightens, realising they are spears.*

He moves sharply, pulling each one from the ground and snapping it in two until he sees WILLIE *at the tent door.*

WILLIE. Be us next time, won't it, Da?

THORNHILL. If they wanted to hurt us we wouldn't be standing here now, lad.

He pulls the last spear from the ground…

It's a show, that's all.

…and throws it onto the fire.

No need to tell your ma about this… Don't want her worrying, do we?

WILLIE *feels caught between being let into his father's confidence and the worry of keeping a secret from his mother. But he nods his agreement… making his choice.*

Get them corn seeds. We'll have 'em in the ground by midday.

Scene Four

Blackwood's Place.

THOMAS BLACKWOOD *sits on a log, coiling a length of rope.*

DHIRRUMBIN. Thornhill found himself with a question and knew only one man who might have an answer. Tom Blackwood. So he took his skiff and, uninvited, he caught the early tide up to the First Branch. Here the river narrows, running through a steep gorge of sheer rock on either side. Aways a way up she opens out into a broad lagoon. A still and silent kind of place. Where a man can hide away if that is his inclination.

THORNHILL *enters. He holds a wrapped parcel of something.*

BLACKWOOD. You've got yourself up here, Will Thornhill. Stickybeaking without no one asking you.

THORNHILL. That's a fine sort of welcome after man rowed five mile.

BLACKWOOD. We are real private up here.

They fall into a silence like men with something on their minds and no clear way to say it often do. Until THORNHILL *remembers his parcel.*

THORNHILL. Sal sent you some johnnycakes.

BLACKWOOD *takes them with a curt nod.*

BLACKWOOD. So you made your move?

THORNHILL. Said I would.

BLACKWOOD. Your missus?

THORNHILL. She'll be happier when a hut's up… I'm doing a run to Sydney end of the week. Anything you need?

BLACKWOOD. Got all I need right here and you didn't row five miles for a shopping list.

THORNHILL. Got a blacks' camp along of me… Come out of the blue.

BLACKWOOD *is silent.*

Just come without so much as a by-your-leave.

BLACKWOOD. They give you a fright, Will?

THORNHILL. Not so much a fright.

BLACKWOOD. Then what?

It's not a question THORNHILL *finds easy to answer.*

They'll move on.

THORNHILL. When?

BLACKWOOD. Soon enough.

THORNHILL. Well, a man doesn't mind having a visitor when he knows the day the visitor is leaving.

BLACKWOOD. You don't see it, do you?

THORNHILL. What?

BLACKWOOD. That they're thinking the same thing.

THORNHILL. I'm not going anywhere.

BLACKWOOD *kicks at the dirt a little. Takes out his pipe. Looks over the water.*

BLACKWOOD. Coming up from Sydney one day early on in what was once called *The Queen*. Not a breath of wind on the river and the tide going out fast. Had to pull ashore. Up round Sandy Island, that bit of beach... blacks there waiting for me.

THORNHILL. Is that right?

BLACKWOOD. They come down, see. Tell me to bugger off. Had their bloody spears up ready. I was shitting myself. It was like they was waiting for something. Give them some food. But they wasn't having none.

He looks away at the red cliffs above them. THORNHILL *wonders if a little prompting might help him back to telling his tale.*

THORNHILL. So what was they waiting for?

BLACKWOOD. Search me, mate, but I took my flaming hat off my head and gave it to one of them. Now a hat, to the likes of you and me, with our fair complexions, is worth something, but to the likes of these it means sweet fuck-all. Do you understand where I'm going with this?

THORNHILL. Can't say I do.

BLACKWOOD. They ain't got no need for what we have. Same can't be said the other way... I hope you come to understand that, Will... Long and short, they let me camp. Made it real clear, though. Stay on the beach. Couldn't have been clearer if they'd spoken the King's English. Had a good old singsong later on up the hill. You know, sticks and that. Kept away like they said. Buggers kept my hat, though.

He laughs at the memory.

Ain't nothing in this world just for the taking. Matter of give a little, take a little. That's the way it's got to be. Know your place. Otherwise you're dead as a flea.

THORNHILL. Just that with me doing the run down to Sydney, Sal and the boys be alone... with them blacks around.

BLACKWOOD. Then they'll be alright then, won't they?… You tell Sal just to get on with her business and stay clear of theirs.

Beat.

You pass Smasher Sullivan's on the way here?

THORNHILL *nods.*

He see you?

THORNHILL. He tried to wave me in… wants a load picked up.

BLACKWOOD. So he knows Sal's there on her own.

THORNHILL *takes this in. The warning clear.*

Best be on your way, Will.

THORNHILL *makes to go when he sees a tar-coloured child standing at the edge of the clearing, watching him. A woman,* DULLA DYIN, *emerges after him. Seeing* THORNHILL, *she cups her hand around the child.*

She speaks. In amongst it, THORNHILL *picks out the odd English word. To* THORNHILL*'s astonishment,* BLACKWOOD *answers her in the same creole language.*

DULLA DYIN. Wanjan dah nanu? [*Who is that one?*]

BLACKWOOD. William Thornhill nanu. He's made camp up river. With his winangadyin [*wife*] and gulyanggarri [*children*].

DULLA DYIN. Ngaya byalla dullai mulla diem. Yan gili, yella-da jillung ni. [*I don't want strangers coming up here. Going back, telling stories about what they seen.*]

BLACKWOOD. He's a good one, this one. Budyari. [*Good.*]

DULLA DYIN. Ngyini byalla nanu yan. Ngmuun ngan nanu ni. Wiri wiri-da guwuwi. [*You tell him to go. And to stay quiet about what he's seen. Or trouble will come from this.*]

DULLA DYIN *retreats with the child, leaving a silence between the men who find themselves without enough words to say what's going on here. Eventually…*

BLACKWOOD. I ask you to keep your trap shut. About what you seen here.

THORNHILL *nods. He remains silent.*

Say something, man.

THORNHILL. Ain't none of my business.

BLACKWOOD. That's right… it ain't. But that woman is a better wife to me than any I had in London.

Scene Five

The Thornhills' Camp.

As the light softens against the cliffs and the day stretches toward the night, SAL *sings 'Oranges and Lemons' as she sweeps her square of dirt clean.* DICK *sings with her as he dreams and whittles at a stick and* WILLIE, *always wanting to do a man's work, prepares the fire.*

SAL *and* DICK (*singing*).
>Oranges and lemons,
>Say the bells of St Clement's.
>You owe me five farthings,
>Say the bells of St Martin's*

Come on, Willie. Cat got your tongue?

WILLIE *joins in, though he secretly thinks he's too old for this.*

ALL (*singing*).
>When will you pay me,
>Say the bells of Old Bailey.
>When I grow rich,
>Say the bells of Shoreditch.

One by one they become quiet as they realise that a fourth voice is singing with them…

SMASHER (*singing as he enters*).
>When will that be?

* See page 104 for musical score.

Say the bells of Stepney.
I do not know,
Says the great bell of Bow.
Here comes the candle to light you to bed,
And here comes a chopper to chop off your head.

He has seized WILLIE *and mocks chopping his head off.*
WILLIE *breaks away. Both boys move to their mother's side.*

SMASHER SULLIVAN *has put on his best for the visit: a*
blue coat with gilt buttons, a little tight under the arms.

It's true then… Word's up and down the river that Will
Thornhill has set up camp with his missus and little-ens.

SAL. My husband's not here.

SMASHER. No? Shame. Got business for him. A load of lime
needs taking to Sydney.

SAL. I'll be sure to tell him.

SMASHER. Sullivan's my name. Smasher Sullivan. Got a place
upriver from here. On Sullivan's Creek, no less. Could say
we're neighbours.

SAL. Pleased to meet you, Mr Sullivan. I'd ask you in but we
ain't got no in.

SMASHER. We all started in the same way, Mrs Thornhill. With a
parlour under the stars. Just like them blackfellas, hey? But I see
you got two sets of extra hands. You'll have this place cleared
and a hut up before you know it.

SAL. You give me a start… coming up out of nowhere.

SMASHER. I called up from the shore. Then I heard the singing.
You and your boys singing songs from home. It warms your
heart to hear one of them old songs.

SAL. Get Mr Sullivan a drink, Willie.

SMASHER. Don't mind if I do.

An anxious glance from the boy, but SAL *reassures him with a*
nod. He moves into the tent to find the Thornhills' precious bottle
of brandy.

SAL. Pull up a log, Mr Sullivan.

SMASHER. Call me Smasher.

> WILLIE *returns with the bottle and a cup.*

SAL. Can't see that being a name your mother gave you.

SMASHER. Wouldn't know. Never knew her. Died pushing me out. Got a vague memory of Arthur being in the picture some time back but been Smasher so long it may as well be what was writ on the certificate.

> SAL *pours him a tot.* SMASHER *downs it and has the cup back ready for a second before she can put the cork back in. She pours him another.*

> Bets being laid how long you'll last out here.

SAL. Oh?... I'll last, Smasher. But five years is my sentence. Then we're going back.

SMASHER. To Sydney?

SAL. No. Home.

SMASHER. London?

SAL. Why not? We had a decent life there.

SMASHER. If it was so decent how come your husband turned lag?

SAL. A bit of bad luck is all.

SMASHER. Oh, yeah...

> *He holds out his cup for another splash. She obliges.*

> Same bit of bad luck I had. Fella caught me with my hand in his pocket. Real bad luck that was. Nah... wouldn't get me going back. I was shit in London. Hungry most days. Here, at least I got a piece of dirt of my own. You ever think that, Mrs Thornhill?

SAL. Sal's my name.

SMASHER. You ever think, Sal, that the likes of us could be standing on dirt that belongs to us? Me? A nasty little sweep

from the East End of London owning something other than
some other man's coat. It makes me want to cry. It does. I could
fucking cry. I wish my old man could see this. I wish he was
here. I'd rub the cunt's face in the dirt. I'd say, here. I own this.

SAL. That'll do.

She indicates the boys.

SMASHER. Sensitive lads, are they?

He reaches and strokes DICK'*s face.*

When I was your age, younger, I was being shoved up the arse-
end of a chimney with my father's boot on my backside.
Youngest of six, I was. Lucky if I saw a scrap at table after my
brothers got there first. Old man happy to keep it that way. Kept
me skinny, you see. All the better to get up them chimneys.

DICK *steps away. The man's touch is not welcome.*

Here, I got no man over me and I take what I want.

SAL. We ain't going back with nothing. We'll work. Make our pile.
Go back with enough to buy something. Nothing too grand.
Place back of Borough Market do me.

SMASHER. You still be just a lag's wife.

SAL. I don't care what I'll be. I'll be home.

SMASHER *holds out his cup.*

You got the taste for it, Smasher.

SMASHER. Don't we all?

*She pours him another. He takes his grog… walks around the
camp, taking it in, what they own, what they don't.*

Nice piece he's grabbed for himself here, your husband.

His slow smile reveals a mouth of rotten teeth.

Had any trouble with the blacks?

SAL. Some come round when we first got here.

SMASHER. Tell your husband to keep a whip at hand. Best thing.

SAL. I don't see no cause for that.

SMASHER. You don't what? You don't see no cause? They're thieving bastards, Sal. They'll take anything not nailed down. And not because they want it. Just for the spite of it. But that's the least of it. You heard what went on up beyond Green Hills at South Creek? Two men scalped alive.

SAL. I never heard that.

SMASHER. In the *Gazette*, no less. And a child taken. Its throat slit. Not to mention what they did to its mother.

SAL. That'll do. Hard enough being out here alone without knowing the likes of that.

SMASHER. Your husband best get himself a gun. Keep it loaded. And a couple of dogs. I'll sell him some, if he wants. Trained 'em well. Tear a blackfella's throat out, get the chance.

SAL. Tide's changing, Smasher. You don't want to miss it. Long row back against the flow. I'll tell Will you called by.

Scene Six

That Night, the Thornhills' Camp.

The night is black… no moon, no stars, no light except for the flame of the fire reflected in SAL's *face.* DICK *is beside her, his head resting in her lap as she runs her fingers through his hair. She tightens at the sound of someone's approach.*

SAL. Will?

THORNHILL (*entering*). You right, love?

SAL. You're late back.

THORNHILL. The river was against me… Had to wait for the tide. Where's Willie?

SAL. Asleep… nothing keeps that one awake at night.

THORNHILL. Dick, lad… time for bed.

SAL. Leave him… Not often he lets me hold him any more.

THORNHILL. You'll ruin him with your softness.

SAL. I been sitting here thinking what happens if you don't come back one day.

THORNHILL. That won't happen.

SAL. Not up to you though, is it? *The Hope* turns over in a gale on the run to Sydney and that's you gone and us up here, not knowing nothing.

THORNHILL. I'd hope you'd take me for a better boatman than that.

SAL *is silent*.

I'll always come back, Sal. Might be a day after I said, maybe two, the wind having a mind of its own, but I will always come back.

SAL. The night was never this dark in London.

THORNHILL. You're in a strange kind of mood tonight.

SAL. A man came by today. Smasher Sullivan. Said something about a load of lime.

THORNHILL. He came here? By himself?

SAL. I know how to handle the likes of Smasher. Besides, not as if we're spoilt for company.

THORNHILL. Better off alone than having Smasher Sullivan as a friend.

SAL. I was alright with him. Until he started on about the blacks… Some business up past Green Hills.

THORNHILL. It's gammon. Take it from me, pet.

SAL. Said he read it in the *Gazette*.

THORNHILL. Well, there you go. Think the likes of Smasher Sullivan can read?

SAL. He boasted of using his whip against them… A man would do that after he's likely felt the end of one himself.

THORNHILL. He ain't a good sort, love.

SAL. You wouldn't do anything like that, would you?

THORNHILL. Is that what you think of me?

SAL. I think the world of you.

THORNHILL. Then you got no need to ask me that.

SAL. Said he had a couple of dogs for sale. If we needed them.

THORNHILL. You see any sign of them?

SAL. Saw their smoke on other side of the point as the sun went down. And when I went to do my business I got a strange feeling someone was watching me. Got such a fright I dropped my hat. When I went back later to get it, it was gone.

THORNHILL. Probably not looking in the right place.

SAL. I walk the path twice a day. Don't stray from it. Reckon I know where it dropped.

THORNHILL. Blackwood says they'll move on soon enough.

SAL. When?

THORNHILL. When they're ready.

SAL. S'pose he's right, with their roaming ways.

THORNHILL. You awake, lad?

    DICK *is silent… asleep or pretending to be.*

    Something I seen up there… at Blackwood's. Got a woman with him. And a child.

SAL. He's a dark horse.

THORNHILL. So is she, pet.

SAL. Never… What, like they shacked up together? Like man and wife?

THORNHILL. We ain't to say anything… others wouldn't see it way we do.

SAL. Doesn't help us though, Will. With our situation. Maybe you should go down and have a talk to them.

THORNHILL. And how do you think I might do that? Them talking their language and me talking mine.

SAL. Worth a try though, ain't it? Just to politely explain that we're here now and we wouldn't mind if they just buggered off somewhere else.

THORNHILL. Maybe I will. Step down and have a word. Get things straightened out.

DICK *pops his head up out of* SAL*'s lap*.

DICK. Can I come, Da?

THORNHILL. You're meant to be asleep… and no, you bloody can't.

Scene Seven

The Dharug Camp.

GILYAGAN *sings as she sweeps a patch of ground clean with a twist of reeds bound together as a broom.* NARRABI *and* GARRAWAY *feed the fire with twigs. It is a mirror image of the Thornhill's own camp.*

GILYAGAN (*singing*).
>Dadjabayalung! Dadjabayalung! [*It's a beautiful day!*]
>Nurawa guwinga guwinga guwinga guwinga. [*We're on country with fire.*]
>Nurawa guwinga guwinga guwinga guwinga. [*We're on country with fire.*]
>Djinmang djinmang djinmang djinmang djinmang djinmang djinmang djinmang [*I'm a married woman*]
>Mullabu wangarra mullabu wangarra mullabu wangarra mullabu wangarra. [*With two boys.*]*

Bark dishes. Berries. Daisy yams. A hollowed stone for grinding seeds. BURYIA, *the old woman, throws a snake on the fire. She wears* SAL*'s cloth cap perched on top of her head. She settles on the ground, takes a stick and covers the snakes with coals as…*

* See page 105 for musical score.

BURYIA. Ngyina bulla-da biyi? [*You two hungry?*]

NARRABI. Yuin. [*Yes.*]

BURYIA. Diya gahn budyari wungal. Yan gunama nanu ngyini dane. [*This snake is a good one. Going to cook him up for you two.*]

GARRAWAY. Ngaya biall ghan. [*I hate snake.*]

BURYIA. Ghan marragawan burbuga-da barrang. [*Well, you can eat snake or you can have an empty belly.*]

GILYAGAN. Ngan ngmuun? Nanu guwuwi. Ngan dullai tullah mullah. [*You hear that?... He's coming. That white man.*]

BURYIA. Ngyina gawi. Murry dana, ngan. Nanu wiri wulbunga-da. Badagarung ngarra. [*We should call him Heavy Foot, that one. He'd be no good at hunting. Kangaroos hear him from a long way. They'd be off before he even knew they were there.*]

The boy's laughter quietens as THORNHILL *enters.* BURYIA *glances up but with little interest, as if he were a fly come to watch them.*

THORNHILL. Well, bugger me, missus, but you're wearing my wife's hat.

Nobody seems to notice that he has spoken. BURYIA *turns the snake over in the fire.* GILYAGAN *sits down beside her and starts twisting a length of twine on her thigh.* THORNHILL *tries a different tack.*

I came down here to say that youse lot better bugger off.

GILYAGAN. Bulla-bu yanira nanu yana. [*You two make yourselves scarce until he's gone.*]

NARRABI. Nanu wurabata wugal. [*I'm not afraid of that one.*]

GILYAGAN. Yuin wurbata dye yenma budyar-yan. [*But you're afraid of me so if you know what's good for you, you'll get going.*]

The boys rise and leave.

THORNHILL. Best stay away. Out of our place.

The words pass, leaving a silence behind them. THORNHILL *takes a bold step forward. Without haste,* BURYIA *rises and stands her ground, the way a tree stands on its piece of earth.*

DHIRRUMBIN. Will Thornhill didn't know where to look. He felt his face burn with shame. He'd never seen a naked woman standing there in front of him. Only Sal and she only in bits and only beneath the blanket. And yet facing this old girl he feels like he's the one wearing no clothes.

BURYIA *flaps her arm at him and begins to speak, brusque and emphatic. She has no fear of him and expects no disagreement.*

BURYIA. Wanjan, ngan diem? Yan wellamabami. Gunan gabara. [*Who are you? What do you want here? You go back to where you came from, you shithead.*]

When she is done she turns away as if shutting a door between them.

THORNHILL. Listen, missus, I could fetch a gun and blow your heathen head off easy as anything.

Something makes him turn. YALAMUNDI, NGALAMALUM *and* WANGARRA *are watching him.*

Good day to you, gentlemen. How are you this fine day?

NGALAMALUM. Wanjan diya binnangarri binnangarri? [*Who does he think he is?*]

WANGARRA. Nanu gadyalang, Baggy barrang. [*He must be hot… wearing all that.*]

NGALAMALUM. Nanu ni gadyalang. Thurrull gabara. [*He looks bloody hot… all red in the face.*]

They laugh. THORNHILL *laughs with them but wonders if the joke might be on him.*

THORNHILL. That's right… we're all friends here, sharing a laugh.

YALAMUNDI *remains above it. Cautious.*

I'm wondering, I was just asking your good woman here. How long, gents, you think you might be staying? Here. On my place.

He hears his words evaporate, thin and silly. A bird begins a long tweeting in the trees above, marking the silence.

Cat got your tongues? You black buggers.

YALAMUNDI *walks towards him and places a hand on his forearm. Authority radiates off the old man like heat off a fire. A stream of words begin to come out of his mouth.*

YALAMUNDI. Ngaya biyal wural, ngyini ngarra ngaya. Yalamundi gugarug. [*I'm not going to hurt you, but you need to listen. I am the law man here. You need to do things the right way.*]

THORNHILL. Very good, old bugger. Now you listen to me... If I may.

He takes a stick and draws a curving line in the dust for the river and a tidy square representing his hundred acres. Inside the square he draws three dots and then joins them up to make a letter 'T'.

This here is the river, yeah? And this? This is mine now. That's a 'T', Thornhill's place. You got all the rest. You got the whole blessed rest of it, mate, and welcome to it. But not this bit. This is mine.

YALAMUNDI *gives a cursory look at the marks in the sand and then proceeds with his own agenda. He takes a handful of the daisy yams.*

YALAMUNDI. Dah biyi, Budyari. Wyabuinya gulyangarri, maana mudang-ga. [*It's food. Good to eat. You give it to your children. Make them strong fellas.*]

He bites one, chews, swallows, nods. He holds one out to THORNHILL.

THORNHILL. Kind of you, old boy. But you keep your radishes. Monkey food I would call that, mate, but good luck to you.

YALAMUNDI. Ininnyah durubin, nura midyini. Gunan guni nura midyini. Gunan guni naur Bumradbanga midyini. Mimadyimi. Wingaru dullai Mawn? [*Down at the river, is the place for the yams. You know that place. You make a big mess of that place. Destroy all the yams. Leave nothing for us. Go dig closer to your camp but leave the place for yams alone. Do you understand what I'm saying, whitefella?*]

THORNHILL *senses the question in the man's tone and nods his head.*

THORNHILL. Yes, mate. You stick to your victuals. And we'll stick to ours.

NGALAMALUM. Byall guyanayalung. Bugu wugal gamay. [*Talk if you want, old man, but this one only knows the meaning of a spear.*]

YALAMUNDI. Ngan Ngalamalum? Bugu wugal ngai nanu wingaru. [*And then, Ngalamalum? You kill this one then ten more like him come.*]

THORNHILL. Just as long as you understand that this place is mine now.

YALAMUNDI. Ngaya nanu wingaru wugal. [*He understands, this one.*]

THORNHILL. And sooner or later you will have to move on. You know that, don't you?

Sensing the question in his tone, YALAMUNDI *nods.* THORNHILL *nods back as though they are both agreeing to the same thing.*

That's good then. We understand one another… You'll be on your way soon then?… So, good luck to ya.

YALAMUNDI. Ngyina diem, jiilung yan, ni. [*We just wait. They'll move on. You'll see.*]

THORNHILL *takes his leave as* NGALAMALUM *approaches and looks down at* THORNHILL*'s map. He wipes it clean with a sweep of his foot.*

* * *

Back at the Thornhills' Camp.

SAL, WILLIE *and* DICK *wait anxiously for his return.*
THORNHILL *enters. He sees their faces wanting the answer.*

THORNHILL. Good as gold… Old feller seemed to get the gist.
    They'll be off again by and by.

*They are all silent. Nobody quite believes him. Least of all
himself.*

Scene Eight

The River Flat.

DICK *stands on the shore of the river.*

DHIRRUMBIN. Dick stood on the shore and watched *The Hope*
    sail away with his father and brother on board. He wondered
    why Willie got to go to Sydney and he had to stay behind to
    look after the corn. Sometimes he wondered if his da liked
    Willie more than him. Once he asked his mother and she told
    him not to be silly. Their da liked them both the same, but
    secretly he knew she had to say that.

Some distance away, NARRABI *and* GARRAWAY *explore a
rock pool with sticks.*

DICK. What are youse two doing?

The boys take no notice of him. DICK *moves a little closer.*

I said what are youse two doing?

NARRABI. Nuna guwuwi. [*He wants to come over.*]

GARRAWAY. Ngyiri nanu, yuin? [*Should we let him?*]

NARRABI. Nah biyal. [*No.*]

DICK. Hey, my name's Dick.

NARRABI. Biyal naala wawa nanu. [*Don't look at him.*]

GARRAWAY. Garranarbilli nanu. [*Funny-looking fella.*]

DICK. What you looking at?

He edges closer.

Can I play?

He edges closer.

The boys are pointing at something in the water. NARRABI *waves him over.*

NARRABI. Guwuwi… naala diya. [*Come over… look at this.*]

DICK's there in a shot. He doesn't need to be asked twice.

DICK. What is it?

NARRABI. Naala ni… minyin. [*Look closer… there.*]

DICK *bends down and peers into the water… a look passes between* NARRABI *and* GARRAWAY – *a secret plan afoot – and then* GARRAWAY *splashes water in* DICK's *face.*

DICK. You did that on purpose.

The Dharug boys bend with laughter. They laugh so much it hurts. Until DICK, *with his dripping face, gives as good as he gets and returns fire.*

And it's on. A big water fight, and in the midst of it the discovery that they can slide across the stage.

Awww… you can slide!

DHIRRUMBIN. They splashed each other until they were soaking wet. They ran until they had no breath. They laughed until their sides wanted to split.

And they did not stop until the sun began to set and they heard their mothers calling: Sal from her side of the point and Gilyagan from hers.

GILYAGAN. Narrabi – Garraway!

SAL. Dick!

GILYAGAN. Gawi Guwuwi Garraway! [*Come over here!*]

SAL. Teatime, Dick!

DHIRRUMBIN. Neither knowing they were calling for the same thing.

Scene Nine

Smasher's Place.

The savagery of snarling dogs. SMASHER *silences them with a vicious command. He stands on the shore watching* The Hope *approach. A load of barrels stand ready for shipping.*

SMASHER (*to the dogs*). Shut up!

DHIRRUMBIN. Sullivan's Creek, as Smasher had named it, was a crooked length of water between high, wooded ridges. In there the sun shone coldly and the water was black as a mirror. Not a breath of wind stirred its glassy surface or blew away the stain of smoke that hung between the ridges.

The fires for the lime burned day and night. The block had been cleared of all timber, used for fuel, and sat like a gash in the forest. He had worked through the empty layers of oyster shells that had lain there for a thousand years, and more. He'd dug out the midden until there was only black mud left. Now he was burning the live oysters, not bothering with the meat inside. The man smelt of burning flesh.

SMASHER. Lime's been waiting more than a week for you, Thornhill.

THORNHILL *and* WILLIE *enter… having walked up from tethering* The Hope *ashore.*

I can always take my business elsewhere.

THORNHILL. That's your choice, Smasher.

SMASHER. You got it all sewn up, ain't you, Will Thornhill? You must be putting away a pretty packet. Nuff to get you and yours back to London. That's the plan, isn't it?

THORNHILL. Lime's not going to load itself.

SMASHER. Is all I'm saying is that this arrangement is good for the both of us. We need each other…

THORNHILL (*to* WILLIE). Can you handle one of these by yourself?

WILLIE. Ya.

WILLIE tries to lift a barrel.

THORNHILL. Not like that. Do your back in. (*Showing him.*) Roll it like. Weight of it do the work for you.

WILLIE gets on with the job as THORNHILL moves for his own barrel.

SMASHER. Have you got any tobacco about you? I would kill for a plug.

THORNHILL hands him his pouch and watches as he cuts off a plug and puts it in his mouth and another in his pocket for later.

Bring me a pouch or two from Sydney. And a bag of that green powder for the vermin… Tell you what, I'll make youse a cup a tea. Your boy here and all.

THORNHILL. Ain't no time for tea, Smasher.

SMASHER. Always time for a cup a tea. Bit of a yarn. A man doesn't see a face the colour of his own here too often.

THORNHILL. I'll miss the tide.

SMASHER. Christ, I'm trying to be civil. Asking for a moment of your time, that's all. A bit of company. Drive a man silly out here. The silence. A friendly word won't cost you much.

THORNHILL sees, behind the man's filthy smile, a well of loneliness he did not expect.

WILLIE returns for another barrel.

THORNHILL. A cup of tea then. But we'll do the load first.

SMASHER. I'll get that billy on. Spot a grub too… for the boy.

Suddenly the vicious barking of the dogs as they strain at the end of their chains. SMASHER wheels around knowing it can only mean one thing. He yells them to silence.

A tall and powerful young man stands at the edge of the clearing – BRANIYAMALA. He holds no spear, only a plump oyster shell the size of his hand with the water still running from it. Once he has their attention he opens it with the twist of his thumbnail. Then he tilts his head back and sucks down the contents.

BRANIYAMALA. Jillung Branyi, bada-da. Biyal guwinga. Yura guwinga. [*These are oysters. You eat them. You don't burn them. Wasting them. They're not for the fire.*]

SMASHER *is not a man who will take a lesson from a black.*

SMASHER. Fuck off, will yer. You're on my land.

BRANIYAMALA. Biyi narang. Gugu ngalium ngaananga, ngai wingaru-da. [*You eat what you need. Leave the rest for us. I'm not asking. I'm telling you now.*]

He does not see SMASHER*'s hand reach for his whip.*

SMASHER. I told you to fuck off.

He flicks the whip, catching BRANIYAMALA *full in the chest, and the black skin blossoms with a long red slash.*

Fuck off.

He lifts his arm to strike again, but with a movement too fast to see BRANIYAMALA *catches hold of the end of the lash. They stare at each other, joined by the whip. A sharp tug pulls it from* SMASHER*'s hand. Then without a word* BRANIYAMALA *lets it go and turns his back on the scene and disappears into the bush.*

That'll show you. You black bastard!

In the shock of the silence that follows, THORNHILL *sees* WILLIE *wipe his eyes with the back of his arm before any tears get a mind to fall.*

THORNHILL. Move that barrel down there and wait for me at the boat.

SMASHER. I'll get that billy on, shall I? (*Off* THORNHILL*'s look.*) What, Thornhill? You got something to say to me.

THORNHILL. You can keep your damn tea, Smasher.

He picks up a barrel and lifts it to his shoulder.

SMASHER. That was nothing. Just a friendly reminder like. There's no other way.

THORNHILL *carries the barrel down to the boat with*
SMASHER*'s voice trailing after him.*

Best get yerself a gun in Sydney… They'll get you one fine
day. You think they won't, you're a bigger fool than I took you
for, Thornhill.

THORNHILL *has gone… and* SMASHER *is alone again. He*
listens to the wind rushing through the trees up high on the ridge
and thinks of a cup of tea and a yarn he could have had.

(*To the barking dogs.*) Get in behind!

Scene Ten

The Thornhills' Camp.

SAL *marks the tree. Near to a month now.* MRS HERRING *sits*
around the fire. She has a pipe stuck fast in her mouth. Her
eyebrow and a patch of hair are stained yellow from the smoke.
DICK*'s at the fire also.*

DHIRRUMBIN. Sal never spoke of her loneliness to Thornhill.
And he never asked in case it led to the obvious. Another woman
would have made her feelings clear. Another woman would have
forced the issue her way. He loved her for not being that woman.
All the same, before they turned toward Sydney, Thornhill took
The Hope up to Cat-Eye Creek to ask the widow, Mrs Herring, if
she wouldn't mind keeping Sal company until he returned. The
old girl knew what it was like to be lonely. So she baked a loaf
of bread, grabbed some fresh eggs from her hens, and rowed her
skiff down to Thornhill Point.

SAL. But aren't you lonely up there at Cat-Eye?

MRS HERRING. At times… It passes.

SAL. What about Mr Herring?

MRS HERRING. Tree fell on him. Broke his back. Lived a
month. Better dead. Not much I could do with him like that.

DICK. Can I go, Ma?

SAL. We got company.

MRS HERRING. Let him go. Boy doesn't want to sit around listening to an old woman all day.

SAL gives him a nod and he's off.

SAL. Get on then. You want to keep that corn patch weeded, Dick. Your father will be looking when he comes back... Don't know where he gets to, that boy... A cup of tea, Mrs Herring?

MRS HERRING. What time is it?

SAL. Not yet midday.

MRS HERRING. Time for a tot then.

SAL pours them both a tot of brandy.

I find it's good for the complexion.

SAL. That it is, Mrs Herring.

They share a laugh until SAL quietens with a thought.

What about them blacks? You being a woman alone.

MRS HERRING. They don't much bother me. They help themselves now and then. I turn a blind eye. Way I see it, I got enough. One old bitch is real cheap to run.

SAL. It's good to have the company of a woman again.

MRS HERRING. You would have liked Sophie Webb, Spider's missus.

SAL. What happened to her?

MRS HERRING. Turned silly in the head. Lost three babes. One after the other. Delivered them myself. All stillborn. Like they didn't want to live. Then the eldest. The one they come with. Bit by a snake. Buried all four of them. All lined up on the hill. Poor little bird, she was – Soph. Went swimming. Would have helped if she knew how. Spider don't go about much now. He don't like to talk about it. Don't imagine he knows how.

SAL *sits quietly in the melancholy of it*.

SAL. I'm expecting myself, Mrs Herring.

MRS HERRING. Thought so. Got a flush in your cheeks give it away. Near three months, I'd say.

SAL. Ain't kept no secrets from my husband but I ain't told him this.

MRS HERRING. Why not?

SAL. Because this one will take its first breath here. And God help me if it takes its last. What then? We bury it in this cold ground. And then what? We go home and leave just a stone to mark the spot. It would kill me to do it. But it will kill me to stay.

She pulls the broken piece of tile from a pocket.

I found this in the sand by Wapping New Stairs on the morning of our last day in London. Just a piece of broken tile. But something at least from home. Had nothing else to bring. Made a promise to myself. I'll take this back by and by. Lay it right back where it came from.

MRS HERRING. Ain't easy to go back. And I'm not just talking about the miles of ocean that must be crossed. England turned its back on you, Sal. Best to let it go.

SAL. I can't… I won't. This place will never be home.

Scene Eleven

Sydney Harbour, on Government Wharf.

THORNHILL *and* WILLIE *watch among the crowd as* CAPTAIN JAMES SUCKLING, *once of the transport* Alexander, *leads a sorry line of chained convicts. Their heads have been carelessly shaved leaving tufts of hair and scabby skin where the shears had bitten too deep.*

DHIRRUMBIN. The *Scarborough* transport lay back against the bright water off Government Wharf in Sydney Cove. Thornhill remembered how it was to be brought up from the darkness and the stench to sunlight, like a white grub revealed in rotten wood.

SUCKLING. I know you.

He flicks about himself importantly with his handkerchief.

Thornhill, is it not? Off the *Alexander* transport.

THORNHILL *nods.*

Do you remember me, man?

THORNHILL. Yes, sir. It's Captain Suckling.

WILLIE *reaches for his father's hand as if to stand as one with him but* THORNHILL *shakes it off, regretting the decision to bring him along so that he could see this.*

SUCKLING. Stand back, for God's sake, man. You harbour the flies so!

THORNHILL *steps back.*

You here for one of these?

THORNHILL. That's right, sir. Got my pardon. Own land now.

SUCKLING. Is that so? A gentleman you pretend to be. Well, a gentleman takes a bath once a week, Thornhill.

THORNHILL *tightens at the insult.*

Go on... strike me. Show your lad the kind of gentleman you are.

THORNHILL *holds himself.*

What's your name, boy?

WILLIE. Willie Thornhill.

SUCKLING. Willie Thornhill what?

WILLIE *looks up at his father, not understanding what is expected of him.*

THORNHILL. You'll address Captain Suckling as sir.

WILLIE. I'm Willie Thornhill, sir.

SUCKLING. Well, Master Thornhill, remember this. You're the son of a common thief. And you always will be… Take your pick, man. Feel free, won't you?

SUCKLING *saunters off.*

THORNHILL *summons himself and works his way down the sorry line of leftovers. One, younger than the rest, looks up at him, squinting through the painful light.*

DAN. Will Thornhill, is it? Will! Dan Oldfield, remember?

DHIRRUMBIN. He remembered well enough. He remembered the hunger they had shared as boys, and the cold, and the way they had stood one day pissing on their own feet, just for the moment's warmth of it.

DAN. It's good to see you, Will. The old place sends its regards. The river ain't the same without our Will Thornhill.

THORNHILL. Forgetting your manners, are you, Dan Oldfield?

He sees the smile on DAN*'s face close down.*

DAN. What!

THORNHILL. It is Mr Thornhill now… You would do well to remember that.

DHIRRUMBIN. As *The Hope* pulled away from the wharf, with Dan crouched below deck and Willie standing bravely at the bow as if he had not seen his father cowed before a better, Thornhill knew that there could be no future for them back in London. On the Hawkesbury a man did not have to drag his past around like a dead dog, and a man's son had no need to call another man 'sir'.

Scene Twelve

The River Flat.

The corn is shin high. DICK *weeds between the rows. He looks up…*

DICK. Ma! Ma!… It's *The Hope*!

SAL. My two sweet Williams!

> SAL *comes bustling down from the camp. She's sees* THORNHILL *and* WILLIE *and is ready to wrap them both in a hug when the sight of the sorry fellow tailing them pulls her up.*

DICK. What have you got?

WILLIE. Heaps of good stuff.

> THORNHILL *carries a newly bought gun wrapped in an oilskin.*

SAL. By God, if it ain't Dan Oldfield. Look at you.

DAN. Why… Sal Thornhill! The best-looking girl on Swan Lane.

THORNHILL. She'll be Mrs Thornhill now.

> *Her eyes search her husband's face, ready to laugh at the thought, but she sees he is serious about this.*

SAL. Yes. It will work out best that way, Dan.

THORNHILL (*to the boys*). Boys, take him up. You can have a feed and then to work.

DAN. As you say… Mr Thornhill.

> WILLIE *and* DICK *lead him away.* SAL *looks to* THORNHILL *for an explanation.*

THORNHILL. We need the labour… and this way when I'm away on the boat there's someone here.

SAL. But, Will… we was all friends as kids.

THORNHILL. We ain't kids no more. And you ain't no lag's wife now, Sal.

SAL. Alright then… if that's the way it needs to be. But you best get that hut built. And mind it has two rooms. 'Cause a man and a woman can't be a husband and a wife with a servant curled up at their feet.

THORNHILL. Jesus, Sal. You're as saucy as you were when you were nineteen.

SAL. You know how I get when I'm in the family way.

A moment.

Yes, Will.

THORNHILL. When will it come?

SAL. Six months or so.

THORNHILL *is silent.*

Once news like that would have made you dance.

THORNHILL. Any trouble while I was away?

He looks off to see the smoke rising on the other side of the point.

SAL. No. Saw the old girl down by the water one day with two boys as old as our own. Had my hand up waving before I even knew what I was doing. Called out hello like I would a neighbour.

THORNHILL. She look at you?

SAL. Not so much at as through, Will. Like I was not even there.

A moment.

Is that what I think it is?

He unwraps the gun.

Do you even know how to use one?

THORNHILL. Can't be too hard.

SAL. Depends what you're firing at, Will.

She turns and walks back to the camp, leaving THORNHILL *alone, watching the smoke rise from the other side of the point.*

YALAMUNDI *and* NGALAMALUM *watching from a distance.*

NGALAMALUM. Ngyina wingaru jillung yan, guyanayalung… jillungiyura wural. [*Do you still think they are going to leave, old man?… These people are here to stay.*]

YALAMUNDI. Ngan biyal manyru. [*I don't know. I don't know.*]

Scene Thirteen

The Thornhills' Hut.

The neighbours have gathered to toast the new abode. And by the sound of the rousing tune being sung, the party is well on its way.

SMASHER is there, he wouldn't miss a party, welcome or not. And MRS HERRING, DAN and LOVEDAY and SAGITTY BIRTLES, who we have not yet met. And the THORNHILLS, of course. SAL's pregnancy is showing in a ripe little bump.

A rousing tune is being sung.

ALL (*singing*).
      I wish I was an apple on an apple tree, an apple tree,
      You'd come by, take a bite of me,
      If I was an apple on an apple tree.
      I wish I had a brandy and a jug of beer, a jug of beer,
      With my arms around my beer,
      Brandy and a jug of beer.
      I wish I was a king and very rich, very rich,
      Give it all up for one little kiss,
      Of your ruby red lips.*

Amongst their cheers, SAL pours another round, beaming with happiness to have company, as LOVEDAY bangs his cup with his spoon.

LOVEDAY. If I may say a word to mark the occasion.

SMASHER. What, another one, you mean?

LOVEDAY. Being a man with a facility for language.

* See page 106 for musical score.

SMASHER. And who doesn't mind the sound of his own voice. Ain't that right, Sagitty?

BIRTLES. What's that?

SMASHER. Loveday… he's full of it.

BIRTLES. Full of it. That's right. Our Loveday. Full of it. As a fat girl's sock.

LOVEDAY. And if our friend, Sagitty Birtles, would put a sock in it long enough, then let's raise our mugs and toast this fine abode. A palace, Mr and Mrs Thornhill. A palace!

SAL. Compared to what we had it is, Mr Loveday.

LOVEDAY. More than just four walls and a roof. 'Tis a message as clear as one written in pen and ink. And the message says that this is mine and I am here to stay.

SAL. Well, for five years anyway.

LOVEDAY. More than just shelter from the elements. A house, my friends, is what marks us as better than them who lack the sense even to clothe their bodies, let alone to put something between them and the night.

SMASHER. You think four walls will stop them? A few bits of wood tied together ain't no barrier to their cunning. Hey, Sagitty?

BIRTLES. That's right. Like weasels. Come into my place once and stripped it bare. Even took the spade I use for shitting.

LOVEDAY. Keep that inside, did you, Sagitty?

BIRTLES. Yes, 'cause I don't trust the bastards.

SMASHER. And don't leave your boots at your door, no matter what the state of them. 'Cause they'll be gone in the morning as sure as the sun rises.

BIRTLES. You remember, Mrs Herring, when they stole Sophie Webb's smalls off the line then she sees them wearing her bonnet and knickers the next day?

MRS HERRING. Aye… and it was the men who was wearing the knickers if I remember right.

LOVEDAY. Took my last two hens that I was keeping...

SMASHER. Knickers and hens is one thing. But when it's the fruit of man's labour.

BIRTLES. Yeah.

SMASHER. A line has to be drawn. A year's wheat. Tell them, Sagitty.

BIRTLES. Bagged up the day before, it was, and carried down to the shore ready for Tom Blackwood to pick up in the *Queen* in the morning. Gone! Spilt most of it in the mud too, the bastards.

SMASHER. Still, learned them a lesson. Ain't done that again.

THORNHILL *sees the smirk pass between* SMASHER *and* BIRTLES.

DAN. What did you do?

SMASHER. Not for this company, lad.

BIRTLES. It's like bleeding flies, ain't it? Kill one, ten more come to its funeral. (*Off* SAL'*s look*.) Oh, I ain't talking killing exactly. Just disperse, like.

SMASHER. They's vermin, same way rats is vermin.

BIRTLES. They'd cut us up like you would a beast. Eat the best bits.

LOVEDAY. Have to boil your bits a good while, Sagitty, before they'd make a meal.

SAL (*seeing the boys wide-eyed with the thought of it*). It's gammon, boys.

SMASHER. Gammon, is it?

THORNHILL. It's loose talk, Smasher. And I've heard enough of it.

MRS HERRING *finally takes her pipe from her mouth*.

MRS HERRING. What one of us does, we all pay for. Do well to remember that, Smasher.

LOVEDAY (*lightening the mood*). Once had a spear in my rear, if you'll pardon the euphony. Took to the bushes to relieve myself.

Lowered my britches and bent to the task when I felt a most unwelcome jab in the behind. Bony I am back there so it bounced off but not without leaving a nasty scar. (*Happy to show them.*) I've still got it.

SAL. Oh, put it away.

LOVEDAY. I have not relieved myself since that day. I will await my return to England where a man can attend to the call of nature without getting a spear up his backside.

They are all relieved to laugh. BIRTLES *hawks up a gob and is ready to spit.*

SAL. You'll take that outside, thank you, Sagitty.

BIRTLES *goes to the door and lets it fly when something catches his eye.*

BIRTLES. Best tie up your dog, Smasher. Tom Blackwood's here.

We hear the savage snarl of SMASHER*'s dog.*

BLACKWOOD. Get down, you bloody mutt!

SMASHER. Missy goes for him, same as if he was one of those black buggers. Funny, ain't it?

A pained yelp and a whimper from Missy suggests BLACKWOOD *has had the best of the altercation.*

SAL *rises to meet him as he appears at the door with a keg of liquor on his shoulder and a box of oranges under his arm as a housewarming gift.*

SAL. Tom Blackwood... ain't it good to see you? Willie, give him a hand.

WILLIE *helps him with the oranges.*

BLACKWOOD. Some oranges off me tree. Keep the scurvy away. And some of my home brew.

SAL. That's kind of you, Tom.

BLACKWOOD. Good for the chest, ain't it, Mrs Herring?

MRS HERRING. It is... and for polishing the silver.

BLACKWOOD *casts a long look around the gathering and doesn't see much to like.*

BLACKWOOD (*by way of greeting*). All.

Nods and 'Toms' come in reply... except from SMASHER.

Them yam daisies down there. Midjini they call them. Midjini. There ain't hardly none left.

THORNHILL. We cleared them out.

BLACKWOOD. They give me a couple when I first come. I gone and give them a nice little mullet for them. Pretty good eating, taken all round, ain't they, Mrs Herring?

MRS HERRING. If you got nothing else.

BLACKWOOD. See, them yams grow where you put the corn. You dig them up, they go hungry. You best share out your crop when it's ready.

SMASHER. Share it! Not fucking likely. They never done nothing. See them breaking their backs to dig in the field.

BIRTLES. We plant where we like.

BLACKWOOD. Do well to know what's growing there first, Sagitty. That's all.

SMASHER. They ain't nothing but thieves. Don't know how to do nothing but thieve off honest men.

BLACKWOOD. Honest men. You ain't never done no thieving, Smasher Sullivan. Oh, my very word, no.

SMASHER *is the only one not laughing.*

You got to work it out your own way. But when you take a little, bear in mind you got to give a little. I'll be off now.

SAL. You'll stay, Tom, to eat. We got a stew of one of Mrs Herring's hens.

BLACKWOOD. All the same... be on my way.

BLACKWOOD *leaves... leaving the mood changed.*

SMASHER. Know what he's going back to, don't we?

A snigger between SMASHER *and* BIRTLES.

SAL. Sing us a tune, Mr Loveday. Something from home.

LOVEDAY. Home.

As LOVEDAY *sings the settlers join him in the melancholy tune 'Little Fishy'.*

The Dharug family are gathered around their own fire: YALAMUNDI, BURYIA, NGALAMALUM, WANGARRA, GILYAGAN, NARRABI *and* GARRAWAY. *They sing their own song of home. It comes from someplace deep…from the past, from the earth. It floats out over the water and up the rise to the shack.*

LOVEDAY *and* SETTLERS (*singing*).
     There's a song in my heart for the one I love best
     And her picture's tattooed all over my chest
     Hey ho, little fishy, don't cry, don't cry,
     Hey ho, little fishy, don't cry.

     The crew is asleep and the ocean's at rest
     And I'm singing this song to the ones I love best
     Hey ho, little fishy, don't cry, don't cry,
     Hey ho, little fishy, don't cry.

     The anchor's a-weigh and the weather is fine
     And the captain's on deck, a-waltzing in time
     Hey ho, little fishy, don't cry, don't cry,
     Hey ho, little fishy, don't cry.

     There are fish in the sea, there's no doubt about it
     Just as good as the ones that have ever come out of it
     Hey ho, little fishy, goodnight, goodnight,
     Hey ho, little fishy, goodnight.*

The Dharug song is sung over the top of 'Little Fish' from after the second chorus and is repeated if necessary to the end of 'Little Fish'.

DHARUG (*singing*).
     Banilung Banilung Banilung Banilung Banilung [*Snapper*]
     Banilung Banilung Banilung Banilung Banilung

* See page 107 for musical score.

Nurada Nurada Nurada Nurada Nurada [*Country*]
Nurada Nurada Nurada Nurada Nurada
Guwuwi Nurada Nurada Nurada Nurada Nurada Nurada
   Nurada [*Calling to country*]
Guwuwi Nurada Nurada Nurada Nurada Nurada Nurada
   Nurada...

The room quietens. And they listen... frightened, bewildered, mystified by this foreign and faraway sound...

... as the Dhurag song rises up over the ridge and fills the valley and the next valley and the next.

End of Act One.

ACT TWO

Scene One

The Other Side of the Point.

In the heat of December, NARRABI, GARRAWAY *and* DICK *are playing a game of 'Grandma's Footsteps' on the bank of the river. Shouts of joy and protest fill the air. (Improvised by the boys according to how the game goes.)*

WILLIE *stands aside, watching from a distance.*

NARRABI. Nuna guwuwi, yuin baban. [*He wants to come over, yes come play.*]

GARRAWAY. Yuin guwuwi yarra da. [*Yes, run over here.*]

DICK. You want to play?

WILLIE. Nah, best go back.

DICK. It's alright.

WILLIE. Ma'll kill us if she knew we were here.

DICK. Ma don't need to know.

DICK *strips his shirt off.*

GARRAWAY. Yuin yan wammalalibyila yagana. [*Yes, let's go swimming together, come away now.*]

NARRABI. Guiwi Dick, guiwi? Nanu budjari. [*Come, Dick, come? He's a good one.*]

DICK. You coming?

WILLIE. Nah.

DICK (*running off*). You're missing out, we're going swimming.

In an instant, DICK *is one of them... his skin white, their skin brown... but all three, running, laughing, in and out, under and up.*

WILLIE *watches… wanting to be one of them, wondering why he can't. He turns and walks away.*

As the three boys swim…

Scene Two

The Thornhills' Camp.

WILLIE *mopes about as* SAL *is busy bringing water back to the camp.*

SAL. Ain't you got chores to do?

> *He shrugs.*

> What's got into you, moping about?

> THORNHILL *approaches with a pile of wood.*

> Well, out with it.

WILLIE. It's nothing.

THORNHILL. Willie… Do I have to come over there?

WILLIE. It's Dick.

SAL. What about him?

WILLIE. He's down with the blacks! Ain't got no clothes on!

SAL. What, none at all?

WILLIE. Right to the skin. With his bum showing and everything else.

> SAL *goes white.*

THORNHILL (*going*). You stay here with ya ma.

Scene Three

The Other Side of the Point.

DICK, NARRABI, GARRAWAY *and* WANGARRA *are
crowded around* NGALAMALUM *as he works on striking a fire.*

*He has split off a bit of dried blackboy stalk, exposing its soft
inside, and has laid it flat on the ground, gripping it with his feet as
if they were another pair of hands. He has fitted a second stick
upright into it, which he is rolling between the palms of his hands
so it twists against the flat one like a drill… beside him is a leaf off
a cabbage tree filled with tinder.*

THORNHILL *enters.*

THORNHILL. Dick!

   DICK *jumps at the sound of his father's voice.*

   Come away from there.

   DICK *approaches.*

   Where's your clothes?

   DICK *points to an old tree stump.*

   Well, put them on. They're not made for hanging on tree stumps.

   DICK *fetches his clothes.*

DICK (*dressing*). He's making a fire, Da. No flint or nothing.

   THORNHILL*'s curiosity gets the better of him and he makes a
   tentative approach.* NGALAMALUM *glances up but makes no
   sign to greet him.* THORNHILL *and the boys crowd in for a
   better look.*

   They watch as NGALAMALUM *works, but there is no sign of
   fire, not even smoke.*

THORNHILL. Come away now.

DICK. Wait, Da – Come and look.

   And then there is smoke… and quick as thought
   NGALAMALUM *tips the sticks into the leaf and wraps the*

*whole thing up, tinder sticks and all into a loose parcel... and
then begins to whirl the package around at arm's length... until,
to their amazement, it burst into flames...*

The boys cheer with delight and DICK *even gives*
NGALAMALUM *a congratulatory pat on his back as he
builds the little fire with sticks.*

And then NGALAMALUM *looks straight at* THORNHILL *with
a grin and a challenge that says 'Match that'.*

NGALAMALUM. Budgari! [*Good!*]

GARRAWAY. Budgari! [*Good!*]

NARRABI. Guwiyang! [*Fire!*]

WANGARRA. Bugari! [*Good!*]

DICK. You did it.

THORNHILL. Well... that's a good trick, ain't it, Dick lad?

DICK. Useful but, Da.

NGALAMALUM. Minga-wa guwinga. [*Put it in the fire.*]

WANGARRA. Yuin. [*Yes.*]

As the boys crowd around the fire, THORNHILL *approaches*
NGALAMALUM.

THORNHILL. I'm his da. You understand? Da. (*Points to his
chest.*) Thornhill. It's my name, get it? Thornhill.

NGALAMALUM *taps his own chest.*

NGALAMALUM. Thornhill.

THORNHILL. Yes! Only it ain't you, mate, it's me that's
Thornhill!

NGALAMALUM *flicks a hand toward him.*

NGALAMALUM. Thornhill.

THORNHILL. Now you've got it.

NGALAMALUM *then places his hand on his own chest.*

NGALAMALUM. Ngalamalum.

THORNHILL. Your what?

NGALAMALUM. Ngalamalum.

THORNHILL. Well, Christ… that's a mouthful.

DICK. It's Ngalamalum, Da. Say it enough and it gets easy.
Ngalamalum.

THORNHILL. All the same I might call him Jack for short,
seeing how he's got such a bleeding mouthful of a moniker.

DICK. And that's Wangarra. He don't say much. Quiet one. And
he's Narrabi. And Garraway. I'm mates with them now.

THORNHILL. Mates, are you?

He holds out his hand to NGALAMALUM.

I'm pleased to meet you, Jack.

NGALAMALUM *steps back from the hand, unsure of*
THORNHILL*'s intent.*

(*Dropping his hand.*) Have it your way, then.

DICK. You should see him throw a spear, Da.

THORNHILL. You're a fine fellow, Jack. I can see that. Even
though your arse is as black as the bottom of a kettle.

THORNHILL *laughs at his own joke.* NGALAMALUM *laughs*
with him until DICK *moves to* NGALAMALUM *and takes the*
man's hand in a gesture of solidarity. THORNHILL *quietens.*

Thing is, mate, you may as well give up now. You see there's
such a bleeding lot of us.

YALAMUNDI *appears and watches from a distance.*

YALAMUNDI. Guwuwi diem yaguna. [*Come away now.*]

NGALAMALUM, WANGARRA, NARRABI *and*
GARRAWAY *depart.*

THORNHILL *and* DICK *watch them go.* NGALAMALUM
looks back and meets THORNHILL*'s eye for a moment before*
leaving.

As the crowds of London pass…

DHIRRUMBIN. Thornhill thought of the crowded streets of London and of the cells of Newgate Prison, where a room built for ten slept fifty and where five hundred rooms like it were all full. He thought of the great wheels of English justice chewing up felons and spitting them out here, boatload after boatload, like he had been spat out, spreading out from Government Wharf, acre by acre, slowed but not stopped by rivers, mountains, swamps. The world here was about to change. The thought of it made him gentle.

Scene Four

That Night, the Thornhills' Hut.

The family sits around the fire, dipping their hard bit of bread into their tea. DAN *takes his place, a little apart from the others.*

SAL. Anything to say, Dick?

He shakes his head.

You wouldn't like to give us some idea of why you were seen dancing around stark naked with them natives today?

DICK. I was swimming, Ma.

SAL. Well, swimming I've never heard the like of. Not by anyone, I know. You ever heard of anyone going swimming by choice, Will?

THORNHILL. No. Never have. Not just for the fun of it.

SAL. But when they do, do you ever hear of the likes of them going naked?

THORNHILL. Never heard of that.

SAL. Think I best take off my skirts and go about like them? Your father strip off his britches?

The thought of it sends WILLIE *into a fit of laughter, but not* DICK, *as if it would be no bother to him if they did.*

THORNHILL. Time you pulled your weight. Not play about with savages.

DICK. They don't need no flint or nothing, like you do. And no damned weeding the corn all day long.

THORNHILL *catches the smirk on* DAN*'s face and feels the rage burst in him. He grabs* DICK *by the arm and drags him away, pulling his belt off as he goes.*

No, don't, no!

SAL *and* WILLIE *wince at the sound of each strike. On the third,* SAL *is on her feet. But she stops herself, knowing that to intervene will make things worse. On the sixth she hears the boy cry out and she has to cover her mouth to stop herself yelling for her husband to stop.*

At last it's over. She can hear DICK*'s muffled sobs as* THORNHILL *returns putting on his belt.* WILLIE *and* DAN *go out to see if the boy is alright.*

THORNHILL. You think I shouldn't have?

SAL. The boy spoke out of turn. You did what a father is expected to do. Just that I think you did it because you didn't like to be shown up in front of Dan Oldfield, like that.

THORNHILL. You think he ought to go about with savages?

SAL. It ain't that. But if he goes about a bit, it's the way you and me did. That place down Rotherhithe, remember? Stealing apples when we could. Getting chased by the owner. Only Dick ain't got no Rotherhithe to go to. He never even heard of the place. This is what he's got. And it's not like we can keep going on, pretending they aren't there.

THORNHILL. Then what?

SAL. I don't know. But maybe we just got to find a way to live with it. Mrs Herring has and Tom Blackwood.

THORNHILL. Just the same, he'll come along with me and Willie on the boat from now on. Do a fair day's work for his dinner. Dan can look after the crop.

Scene Five

The River Flat.

The corn stands high in the summer sun. DAN, *not one for work, leans on his spade and stares up to the ridge above, brushing the flies from his face.*

THORNHILL *comes down from the hut.*

THORNHILL. Looks real easy, don't it, only fifty mile back to Sydney.

DAN *starts back to work.*

You got me down here. Or the forest and the savages out there. Up to you. No skin off my nose.

DAN. Heard stories on the boat over. Of felons wandering into the bush, chancing a walk to China. Never heard of again.

THORNHILL. That's the place it is.

DAN. Thing is, Will – (*Catching himself.*) Mr Thornhill. You and I started the same. Now look at us. You up there. Me down here… How long it take you to get your ticket?

THORNHILL. Two years… and don't think I didn't work for it. And pardoned in another two. Do the work of an honest man, Dan. And you might end up being one.

DAN. Honest man? Been a thief since I was a babe. Stole the milk from me mother's tit from me little brother. Shoved him off and latched on meself. He died. I lived. That's the kind of man I am… Mr Thornhill.

DAN *starts back with his digging.*

Scene Six

The Bush and the Rise Above the Hut.

DICK *is rubbing one stick against another like he has seen* NGALAMALUM *do. He's so concentrated on the task he doesn't hear his father's approach.*

THORNHILL. Do I got to get the belt out again?

DICK *freezes… You hit your child once, deserved or not, he'll never feel quite the same way about you again.*

Just joking, lad. If one beating don't stop you, another won't do it neither. That's one lesson my old man never learned.

DICK *is silent… still distrustful.*

Let's try this savage's trick.

He gets down…

Here, hold this one tight… You just rub it, right?

DICK. Yeah, in here.

DICK *holds the base stick while* THORNHILL *starts to twist the other between the palms of his hand… until the blood starts to pound in his head.*

THORNHILL. Me bloody hands are burning, not the bloody stick.

DICK. Here, Da, give it here.

DICK *takes over but still there is no smoke.*

THORNHILL. Must be some trick to it, lad… You best get that Jack to show you again.

DHIRRUMBIN. It was the closest Thornhill could get to an apology and Dick took it for what it was, permission to be among the blacks. After they tired of the rubbing and with their hands red and burning, Thornhill said he had something he wanted the boy to see. He led him through the bush where there was now the beginnings of a track due to Thornhill having walked it so many times. They climbed up through the trees to the rise above the hut and stood on the flat platform of rock looking over what he called Thornhill Point.

THORNHILL. Look at this, son. You can see the river both ways from here. How it turns this way and that, fattens here, narrows there. Where it's deep. Where it's shallow. How it's run for all them years, chipping away at them cliffs. You got the whole lay of the place here, boy. One day we will build our house up here. And not just a thing of bark. A house made from stone. With rooms for all. A parlour. A sitting room. A fireplace in every room. And here… a place to sit and watch the river pass… Only don't tell your ma. She don't see it yet.

But DICK *has his eyes to the ground, following a honey ant as it crawls over rock. The ant leads him to a line freshly scratched in the rock.*

DICK. Look here, Da.

THORNHILL *pulls himself away from his reverie and comes over.*

Look at them lines.

THORNHILL. That's the way nature works it, water forms a groove in the rock. Runs this way and that.

DICK. Well… looks like them lines all join up to make a fish.

THORNHILL. What fish?

DICK. Look here, Da… here's its spine and a tail.

They walk the length of the carving and at the end of it discover another.

Oh, and look, there's a boat. It could be *The Hope*. And it's even got a line for the tiller at back.

THORNHILL. Ain't no boat.

DICK. All it's missing is you, holding that tiller.

DHIRRUMBIN. He thinks of them up here, making their marks in the rock, at his place, looking out over his point, seeing what he sees.

THORNHILL. It ain't no boat.

He turns and walks away.

Scene Seven

The Thornhills' Camp.

SAL *is at work mixing a damper when she looks up to see*
BURYIA *and* GILYAGAN *watching her.* GILYAGAN *holds a
carved carrying dish full of berries and bush fruits.*

SAL. Bloody hell! (*Calling.*) Will?

The women don't move.

BURYIA. Byalla yarndi nanu Gilyagan. [*Say something to her.*]

GILYAGAN. Ngan ngai byalla? [*What should I say?*]

SAL. You give me a fright… Come visiting, have you? My name
is Sal.

GILYAGAN. Dye giyara Gilyagan. [*I'm Gilyagan.*]

SAL. Beg yours?

BURYIA. Maana bunmarra Nanu. [*Give her those.*]

GILYAGAN. Ngan buun biyi? [*What are we going to eat?*]

BURYIA. Yan-wa. [*Go on.*]

GILYAGAN. Wyanbuininya maana damang. [*Please bring that
bag over here.*]

GILYAGAN *approaches and holds out the berries and fruits to*
SAL. SAL *goes to take the bowl holding them.*

SAL. Oh! Very kind of you.

But GILYAGAN *shakes her head and indicates that she wants
to pour them out.* SAL *finds a plate and holds it out as*
GILYAGAN *pours the bush tucker into it.*

What… you eat these, do you?…

GILYAGAN. Yuin. [*Yes.*]

SAL (*trying them*). Mmm, tasty. (*She's being polite.*) Suppose
you'll be wanting something…Take a seat, hang on a minute.

She fetches a twist of sugar from their supplies.

Here you are.

GILYAGAN *takes it.*

BURYIA. Ngan dah? Ngyiri. [*What is it? Bring it here.*]

GILYAGAN *takes it to the old woman. They both taste it.*

GILYAGAN. Mmmm. Marrinmara? [*Like honey?*]

BURYIA. Budyari. [*Better.*]

GILYAGAN. Dane wangarra. [*Save it for the boys.*]

SAL. Sugar. It's called sugar.

GILYAGAN. Sugar.

SAL. You like it?

BURYIA. Ni naa nanu ininnyah. [*Find out if she's a woman under there.*]

GILYAGAN. Biyal ngan, ngyini da. [*No! I'm not doing that. You do it.*]

BURYIA *approaches and tries to lift* SAL's *skirt.*

BURYIA. Diem murray dah. [*There's more of it.*]

GILYAGAN. Wanjan nanu mulla yan? [*How does her man get through all that?*]

SAL. What are you up to? Stop that! I got just the same as you down there.

BURYIA *squeezes* SAL's *breast.*

Oi!

BURYIA. Nanu dyin. [*She's a woman.*]

SAL. Cheeky old bird… Can't think what's so funny. Here…

BURYIA *feels the cloth of the skirt… she tugs it a little.*

It's my skirt?…

BURYIA *starts to pull it off.*

Oh no… you can't have that… wait… no… oh, alright, then… Tell you what: I give you. You give me. (*Pointing to the carved carrying dish.*) What about that?

BURYIA. Yuin. [*Yes*.]

SAL. Fair exchange.

> BURYIA *nods*. GILYAGAN *doesn't want to give the dish up but* BURYIA *insists*. SAL *slips off her skirt. The women stare at her skirt*. BURYIA *wraps it around her waist*.

> It looks very pretty on you, Meg. You don't mind if I call you that, do you? And how about Polly, for you? Got a friend back home called Polly on Swan Lane.

> BURYIA *walks with a sway making the skirt swing. Then lifts it higher so that it hangs from her shoulders*.

> Well, that's another way to wear it, I suppose.

GILYAGAN. Guwuwi-wa ngai ngarra Murry dana. [*Come on... I can hear that one with the heavy foot coming*.]

> GILYAGAN *and* BURYIA *are laughing as they move away.* SAL *follows...*

SAL. Where are you going... wait on.

> THORNHILL *enters at a rush*.

THORNHILL. What they want?

SAL. I've had a visit?

THORNHILL. Where's your skirt?

SAL. I traded it, Will. Look, for this. Ain't it an oddity?

> *She shows him the dish.*

THORNHILL. You traded your skirt for a piece of bark. What's the use of that?

SAL. Will, you blessed dingbat, it ain't to use, it's a curio. Mrs Herring says gentry pay good money for them kind of things, back home. I get one a month for five years, we'll make a pretty penny when we go back.

THORNHILL. If you start giving they'll be want, want, wanting.

SAL. Buck up with your long face, now.

She wiggles her hips a little.

When's the last time you saw your wife without her skirt on.
You should be a happy man.

THORNHILL. I suppose I could be.

He takes her by the hips.

SAL. Where are the boys?

THORNHILL. Off somewhere.

SAL. And Dan?

THORNHILL. Down at the corn patch.

SAL. Best make it quick then.

* * *

The Bush Nearby.

DICK *meanders like he's killing time as* WILLIE *passes on his
way back to the camp.*

DICK. Best not go in there.

WILLIE. Why not?

DICK. Because Da's dancing with Ma again and they both got
their britches down around their ankles.

Scene Eight

The Thornhills' Camp and the Dharug Camp.

The Dharug are burning the landscape.

YALAMUNDI *walks ahead, giving instructions to the party
behind.* NGALAMALUM *walks with a fire stick, lighting tufts of
grass here and there.* BURYIA, GILYAGAN, WANGARRA,
NARRABI *and* GARRAWAY *walk behind, holding leafy green
branches. Whenever the flame flares they beat it until it subsides.
It is like a kind of dance.*

THORNHILL *is the first to emerge from the hut; the smell of smoke thick in his nostrils, swirling in the air above. One by one they emerge –* DAN, SAL, WILLIE *and* DICK.

DAN. They're burning us out.

WILLIE. Get the gun, Da. Get the gun

SAL. There's no need for that… Will?

DHIRRUMBIN. They watched the fire moving up the slope toward them, but this was not the wild animal of flame that they made when they burned their cleared timber. This was a different thing, a small tame thing that slid from tussock to tussock, pausing to crackle and flare for a moment and then licking tidily on.

With a swift move, GILYAGAN *strikes something with a stick and bends to lift a spotted lizard. With an unhurried move she shakes it until it hangs limp in her hand.*

GILYAGAN. Naa-ni Bunmurra. [*Look what I got.*]

BURYIA. Murrai-marri-da Bumurra. [*Real big one, that one.*]

GARRAWAY. Bunmurra wiri-na. [*I hate lizard.*]

WANGARRA. Ngyini dullai-mulla? [*You a whitefella, then?*]

GARRAWAY. Biyal binangarri. [*No way.*]

The THORNHILLS *stand at the hut wanting to be let into the joke.*

DAN. Jesus Christ… they're going to eat that.

DICK. Lizard tastes real good.

NARRABI. Budgari! [*Good.*]

SAL. Oi, Polly, what are youse all up to? (*Waves.*) Poll!

But they don't look up. It seems as though the part of NSW on which the Thornhills' hut was built is invisible to them.

She don't know her name's Polly, that's all… I give her that name but she don't know that.

SAL *wants to believe it.*

YALAMUNDI. Guwuwi guwinga-da wugal. [*Alright... leave it now... let it burn out.*]

They turn away and disappear back into the bushes from which they came.

DHIRRUMBIN. They had finished what they had come to do and knew that the shape of the place would put the fire out. The Thornhills looked on, trying to understand the meaning of such a show.

DAN. They burned the place for a couple of lizards. They just ain't got no sense.

Rain.

DHIRRUMBIN. The next day it rained. Solid. For two days. Not the wild downpour they had become used to but a soft drizzle that reminded them of home. They stood bareheaded in the wet and for a moment felt blessed.

Then the heat returned and overnight the burned patch turned from black to green. You could almost see the grass growing. And with the tender green came the buru, the kangaroos. Swarms of them. It was like the whole thing was planned.

A mob of kangaroos graze and scratch and lie in the sun.

SAL*'s into the hut and out again with the gun.*

SAL. Here you go, Will, mind you don't shoot your foot off.

THORNHILL *takes the gun, an entirely unfamiliar object to a man of his class. He creeps forward... he raises the gun to his shoulder.*

DICK. That one, Da. That big fella.

SAL. Sssh.

DHIRRUMBIN. The roo was so close he could hear the sound of it tearing at the grass with its mouth. He could see a fly dancing around its ears. He could see the curl of its eyelashes.

An almighty boom as THORNHILL *fires the gun. They all jump back with the fright of it. The recoil was a blow into his shoulder, and he staggers back, blinded by the flash.*

The smoke from the gun clears leaving a silence full of hope as their eyes search for the fallen beast. But gradually the hope fades from their faces.

As the 'bigfella kangaroo' rises to his feet and makes a dignified exit.

WILLIE. You missed it, Da.

THORNHILL. Sometimes, Willie, you got a knack for stating the bleeding obvious.

DAN. Do you smell that?

SAL. It's meat… roasting meat.

DICK. It's kangaroo.

SAL. I don't care what it is… smells like a fine dinner to me.

Their mouths fill with spit. Their tongues run across their lips. Their bellies rumble with emptiness.

DHIRRUMBIN. Just a tail would do. A savoury brown kangaroo stew that would fill a belly the way salt pork never quite did.

THORNHILL *goes into the hut and returns with a bag of flour.*

THORNHILL. Wait on… I won't be long.

* * *

The Dharug Camp.

The Dharug family are gathered around a pit of coals… a roo roasting beneath the embers. The women work at the coals, shifting them this way and that.

BURYIA. Badagarung-wa gwiyanga. [*Put that kangaroo in the fire.*]

GILYAGAN. Ngai ngarra Murry dana. [*I can hear that one with the heavy foot coming.*]

BURYIA. Dullai mulla. Wiri-da. Biyal wulbunga-da. [*That white man. I don't like him. He's not a very good hunter.*]

NGALAMALUM. Ngina-biyi dyinmang, gulyangarri wiri mulla-bu. [*He depends on us to feed his wife and children, bad husband too.*]

THORNHILL enters – the calico bag absurdly white against so much that was dark – skin, earth, wood, stones. He holds the bag up.

THORNHILL. Fair exchange, old boy.

But they pay him no heed until he is left feeling foolish holding the bag up.

YALAMUNDI. Ni ngan jillung maana. [*Find out what he's got.*]

NGALAMALUM *approaches… and takes the bag.*

THORNHILL. It's a knot, you have to untie it.

THORNHILL's *hand reaches to show him how to untie the knot but there is no need.* NGALAMALUM *understands the nature of a knot. He takes it over to* YALAMUNDI.

It's good flour.

The old man reaches in and takes a handful of flour. He smells it, tastes it with the tip of his tongue and shows it to BURYIA. *She glances at it and nods.*

YALAMUNDI *flicks his hand toward the dead roo.*

The tail will do us… or a nice piece of flank.

YALAMUNDI. Yabuininya ininyah binning. [*Get him the bottom of the leg.*]

NGALAMALUM *approaches the dead roo and cuts off a foot. He presents it to* THORNHILL… *a gnarled foot with claws of brown horn and the sinewy first joints.*

THORNHILL. Not the bit I would have chosen, Jack.

NGALAMALUM. Ngyiri dah, Thornhill. [*Take it or leave it, Thornhill.*]

* * *

The Thornhills' Camp.

The THORNHILLS *and* DAN *are still a miserable lot as they sit around the fire – each with their own plate – sifting through the hair and gristle of their dinner.*

DHIRRUMBIN. Skinning the foot of a kangaroo was a harder job than a man would have thought. If it had have been a sheep, the skin would have peeled back like a sock. But with this lump of wood-like meat the skin was glued to the sinews beneath. Eventually Thornhill took to it with an axe. The lumps he dropped into Sal's pot were all fur and bone and gristle. They ended up with a kind of soup with a scum of hair on the top and lumps of bone and strings of sinew gone like bootstraps.

SAL. They won't never believe it back home. That we eaten kangaroo!

THORNHILL. Not so much eat, Sal. More like we drunk kangaroo.

DICK *is the first to laugh… which sets* WILLIE *off and then* SAL *sees the light side of it and then* DAN *has a chuckle. Even* THORNHILL *finds himself with a smile on his face.*

Scene Nine

The Thornhills' Hut.

SAL *is lying in the bed.* MRS HERRING *is sitting at her bedside sewing a decoration onto a white cloth.*

DHIRRUMBIN. One day late in January as Thornhill returned from Sydney, he came round the bend in the river and turned *The Hope* to shore when he saw Dick running down to the water. It was the way the boy was running. There was no joy in it. Just fear.

DICK. It's Ma!

THORNHILL *enters.*

MRS HERRING. Took ill three days back. Your man Dan fetched me. She ain't said a word or taken a thing to eat.

THORNHILL. Is it the child? Because ain't there something you can do? Better to lose it than her.

MRS HERRING. She ain't got the strength for it… The child will come on its own or stay its term. Not up to us.

THORNHILL. What's that you're sewing?

MRS HERRING. Something pretty to wrap her in... if we lose her.

THORNHILL. You'll take that out of here... I don't want to see it again.

MRS HERRING *rises*.

MRS HERRING. That one Blackwood's got up at his place. Best bring her to have a look.

DHIRRUMBIN. But he didn't go. He was too afraid to leave her. And besides, he didn't know how to ask for help from one of them.

THORNHILL *takes a seat by the bed*.

He sat by her side for three days, wiping her brow and wetting her lips with a teaspoon of water. The boys slept at the door. Each night he listened to them crying themselves to sleep. But he had nothing to give. Not a word to soothe them. His eyes never left her.

THORNHILL. When I first met you I couldn't even write my name. You taught me how. You drew the dots on a page and told me to join them. I couldn't even hold the quill. My hand only knew how to hold an oar. But you bent my fingers until they did the job and you steadied my hand as it moved from dot to dot. And there they were like magic. Two letters that stood for me. 'W–T'.

SAL. I think the 'W' was beyond you, Will. But you managed the 'T' alright. Two straight lines, that's all. One standing up...

THORNHILL. And one lying down... I'm sorry.

SAL. For what?

THORNHILL. For the theft that brought us here.

SAL. You had a choice, did you? I don't remember there being none. I remember boiling a bone we found outside the knacker's yard for dinner. And you not having none so there'd be more for the boys... Bury me facing home, Will.

THORNHILL. There'll be no talk of burying.

* * *

The Thornhills' Camp.

With THORNHILL *and the boys at* SAL*'s side, the neighbours
arrive... and gather outside.*

DHIRRUMBIN. News travelled fast along the river. Smasher
rowed up with a couple of mangrove crabs in a wet sack.
Sagitty brought a bit of hog belly fresh killed that day. And
Loveday brought a pumpkin because that's all he had. Useless
thing, a pumpkin, at a time like this. Sal touched none of it. The
woman was wasting away.

DAN. Best-loved girl south of the river. Turned heads, she did.
Not just because of her sweet look but because she had a smile
and a 'Hello' for all she passed. No matter how low they were.

He lowers his voice so that THORNHILL *cannot hear.*

Could have had any man for a husband. Even some that were
her better. We all thought it. Instead she falls for Will Thornhill.
Wild, he was. Look at him the wrong way and you were dead.

SMASHER. He's still the same. Tries to pretend he's not but
scratch the surface and you see it. A bastard made mean by life.

LOVEDAY. Just like the rest of us.

DAN. You know what his old man did for a living? Scraped
dogshit from between the cobbles and sold it to the Morocco
yard. Lower than low, they were. He treats me like shit but I
know who he is and where he comes from.

They rise as one on the sound of an approach. BLACKWOOD
enters with DULLA DYIN *behind. She hangs back at a distance,
wary of this posse of white men.*

SMASHER*'s lip curls.*

SMASHER. What's this?

BLACKWOOD. This is not your business, Smasher.

SMASHER. Who is that bitch?

He reads BLACKWOOD*'s face.*

This your gin, Tom Blackwood? Always wondered why you
had the smell of the black about you.

BLACKWOOD. You going to stand aside, Smasher?

SMASHER. You take your bitch away. We ain't got no need for her.

THORNHILL *appears – a choice before him.*

BIRTLES. You're not going to let her touch Sal, are you, Will?

THORNHILL. Shut your mouth, Sagitty... Now all of you take yourselves home.

They are slow to move.

Do I have to get my gun?

LOVEDAY *and* BIRTLES *trail away.* SMASHER *is the last to move but not before he takes a long look back.*

THORNHILL *leads* BLACKWOOD *and* DULLA DYIN *and* MRS HERRING *inside.*

DULLA DYIN *feels* SAL's *face with the back of her hand.*

Ask her what's wrong with her.

BLACKWOOD. Give her some room, Will. Stand back, all of you.

DULLA DYIN *reaches into her dillybag and takes out something black and slimy.*

THORNHILL. What is that?

BLACKWOOD. Burra. Eel.

THORNHILL. Is this some kind of magic?

BLACKWOOD. More like common sense, I'd say.

DULLA DYIN *strokes the side of* SAL's *mouth like a mother does a baby to ready it for the breast.* SAL's *mouth opens and the woman holds the black flesh to her lips.*

Her eyes open at the salty taste of the raw flesh.

DHIRRUMBIN. Sal saw the face of the woman feeding her but she didn't pull away with fright. She saw in this face a woman she could trust. She sucked on the raw flesh like a child would suck on a sweet. The woman sat with her through the night, feeding her the eel from her own hand. Only a part of Sal was there. The rest was back in London, in her childhood bed with her mother holding pieces of bread soaked in milk as she nursed her through some childhood illness. To be cared for. To be truly cared for. And this woman a stranger to her.

As the light of dawn spreads across the ground and spills into the hut, DULLA DYIN *leaves the bedside and goes outside.*

BLACKWOOD *leans over the sleeping* SAL.

BLACKWOOD. Bit of colour coming back into her cheeks. What do you say, Mrs Herring?

MRS HERRING. If there is… it's the colour green.

BLACKWOOD. Back home my mother did eel in jelly. Best way, she reckoned. Eastcheap. Grantley Street. We lived. There by All Hallows.

SAL. I know it. Stickley's draper round the corner.

They all look. She is weak but she is back.

MRS HERRING. Ah.

BLACKWOOD. That's the one, Sal.

WILLIE. Ma!

SAL. The Tin Whistle Tavern two doors down. Mr Pearly's button store next to that… Will?

THORNHILL *takes her hand, forgetting his own strength.*

I ain't no oar, Will. Leave off.

But he doesn't let go. The boys jump up on the bed, each side of her.

How long 'ave I been lying here like a lump?

WILLIE. Five days, Ma.

SAL. Did anyone make the marks on the tree, or have you all gone and lost track?

DICK. We done 'em on Sunday. Look.

THORNHILL *moves outside. He breathes. He gives a silent thanks and then sees the woman waiting for* BLACKWOOD.

He approaches. He can barely look at her.

THORNHILL. I owe you my thanks.

She gives a curt nod but does not look at him. He clumsily reaches into his pocket and holds out some coins.

Here.

She does not even acknowledge them.

There must be something I can do for you?

DULLU DYIN. You can go, William Thornhill... out of our place. Wurrawa.

THORNHILL. I can't.

Scene Ten

A Black Night, the Thornhills' Hut.

The THORNHILLS *and* DAN *are gathered in silence. They can hear the distant sound of singing and clapsticks coming from the other side of the point.*

DHIRRUMBIN. It was late in the month of February when things began to change. A big mob had gathered at the point. They came down from the ridges in groups, the men walking ahead with the women behind, most with bubs on their hips. Thornhill gave up counting their number at forty. They had got used to the ones they knew; Polly and Meg and Jack and the old man, Whisker Harry, as they called them. But this was something else. Thornhill sensed that they needed to be ready. But ready for what, he was not sure.

SAL. Just having a bit of a get-together. Same as we might ourselves. Might be a wedding or something, don't you reckon, Will?

THORNHILL. A wedding sounds right.

DAN. Don't sound like no wedding to me. Sounds like a fucken war dance.

WILLIE. Get the gun, Da, whyn't you get the gun?

DICK. Ain't no call for the gun. They just having a get-together like Ma says.

WILLIE. Bloody bulldust that is, we got to get the bloody gun.

THORNHILL. Shut it, both of youse.

DAN. I got a knife here. Them buggers come close they get it in their black guts.

THORNHILL. I said shut it.

THORNHILL *rises*.

SAL. Best you don't go out, Will.

WILLIE. Best you don't, Da.

SAL. Will.

THORNHILL *leaves*.

* * *

The Dharug Camp.

Firelight illuminating the trees from beneath, flickering on the skin of the trunks, making a cave of light. Black figures passing in dance in front of the fire.

They are striped with white, their faces masks in which their eyes move. NGALAMALUM, WANGARRA, GARRAWAY, NARRABI *among the many, feet stamping in the dust, no longer men but kangaroos made human.* YALAMUNDI *at the side, telling the story in song.*

YALAMUNDI (*singing*).
     Buruberongal da, Buruberongal da. [*The land where the big old red kangaroo lives.*]

YALAMUNDI *rises… the other men start a different beat with the clapsticks as the old man dances alone, his feet stamping into the ground, so that the dust flies up around him, glowing with light; the pounding of his feet seems like the pulse of the earth itself.*

The Dharug cast sing.

'Garabari song'.

DHARUG (*singing*).
> Buruberongalda! Buruberongalda! [*The land where the big old red kangaroos belong!*]
> Buruda buruda buruda buruda buruda buruda [*That kangaroo, that kangaroo*]
> Badala gunamaga gunamaga gunamaga gunamaga [*Let's eat/cook kangaroo*]
> Burawan murjal buruberongda buruberongda buruberongda [*Jump up kangaroo*]
> Burawan murjal buruberongda buruberongda buruberongda buruberongda. [*See the red kangaroo go up, up.*]*

DHIRRUMBIN. He saw them gathered in the night, their faces lit by fire. A hundred of them. Maybe more. And with each stamp of their feet, with each cry in the night, their power was clear.

Thornhill had let himself believe that there was a way for them and him to be here at the same time. But now something had changed. He saw how a few had become many so quick. And it terrified him.

They dance… the singing fills the night.

Scene Eleven

Smasher's Place.

The savage barking of SMASHER*'s dogs as* THORNHILL *comes up from the river and finds* SMASHER *waiting for him.*

SMASHER (*to the dogs*). Shut up.

THORNHILL. Want to buy a couple of dogs off you.

SMASHER. Starting to see it my way, Thornhill.

THORNHILL. Couple of bitches, five pound, take it or leave it.

* See page 108 for musical score.

SMASHER. Thing is, with the trouble there's been of late, a lot of call for my dogs just now. I could say not less than ten pound, Will, and cheap at the price.

THORNHILL. Five, Smasher. It's my last word.

SMASHER. Call it six then. Got to stick together. One white man to another. Call it six… and I'll let you have a go at this as well.

SMASHER leads THORNHILL up to the hut. Darkness beyond the door. The clink of a chain, the sound of breathing, not SMASHER's or his own.

(*Pulling on a chain.*) Get your idle black arse out here.

He yanks a chained woman out of the hut, MURALI. She shields her eyes from the light, having been kept inside the hut for some time.

Black velvet… only kind a man's got round here. She done it with me and Sagitty. Back and front like a couple of spoons. And your man, Dan, give us a shilling for a go.

THORNHILL *stares at the woman.*

You game, Thornhill? Only watch out, she got claws like a poxy cat.

She looks up at THORNHILL. Her face saying one thing: 'Help me.'

Go on. No one needs to know. You know you want it.

A moment when THORNHILL almost could. And then he turns and walks away.

(*Going after him, dragging the woman with him.*) What? Too good for a piece of free fanny, are you? Good enough for the rest of us, good enough for your mate Tom Blackwood.

DHIRRUMBIN. As he boarded *The Hope* and turned for home, he thought of the woman… He had imagined it. It was no more than a single hot instant; the animal in him. Smasher knew it was there… He tries to believe that he is a better man and yet he doesn't turn the boat around. He left her there and sailed on, wondering if a man decides that he did not see a thing… whether he could make it true.

Scene Twelve

The Thornhills' Camp.

SAL *and* MRS HERRING *outside the hut. As* THORNHILL
enters…

SAL. Been trouble, Will.

MRS HERRING. Up at George Twist's place. Burned him out.
Got himself up to Windsor to tell the tale. A reprisal party been
sent out.

THORNHILL. Jesus Christ.

SAL. What will they do?

Beat.

MRS HERRING. Twist is a fucker of man. Hogs killed his
youngest boy. He saved himself the cost of the burial.
Reckoned the hogs might as well finish what they had started.

THORNHILL. Best stay with us. Until things settle down.

MRS HERRING. Won't settle down. Not now. Something done
to them. Something done to us. That's how it goes.

Scene Thirteen

The Thornhills' Camp.

The settlers are gathered at the Thornhills' place – THORNHILL,
SAL, *the boys,* DAN, MRS HERRING, BLACKWOOD,
LOVEDAY, BIRTLES *and* SMASHER.

DHIRRUMBIN. One by one they sailed down to Thornhill Point.
A proclamation had been made by the Governor and published
in the *Gazette*. All very well but useless if you could not read.
Loveday was the only man on this part of the river with the
vocabulary to manage it.

LOVEDAY (*reading*). 'March the 22nd, 1814. The black natives of the colony have manifested a strong and sanguinary spirit of animosity and hostility towards the British inhabitants.' Meaning they stick a spear in you any chance they get.

BLACKWOOD. Just read the poxy thing, will you?

LOVEDAY (*reading*). 'On occasion of any native coming armed, or in a hostile manner without arms, or in unarmed parties exceeding six in number, to any farm belonging to British subjects, such natives are first to be desired in a civil manner to depart from said farm.'

SMASHER. Civil manner on the end of my gun.

LOVEDAY *holds up his hand to indicate there is more.*

LOVEDAY (*reading*). 'And if they persist in remaining thereon, they are to be driven away by force of arms by the settlers themselves'… Put plain, we may now shoot the buggers whenever we damn well please.

MRS HERRING. Give it here… give it along here to me.

MRS HERRING *and* SAL *bend over the paper, tracing their fingers along the lines, not believing what they have just heard.*

SMASHER. Fuck that one-at-a-time shit.

BIRTLES. Give 'em a dose of the green powder. Sort that mob out at Darkey Creek. They're the ones that stole my wheat.

SMASHER. Think I need any bit of paper from the damned Governor?

He pulls something out of his pocket and throws it on the table. It looks like two bits of leather tied together.

What's mine is mine and I ain't never waited for no by-your-leave.

SAL. What's that?

SMASHER. Ears, Sal. Two of them. Cut 'em straight from the head of one of them black buggers.

DICK *screams.*

SAL. Get them out of here... get them out!

SAL drives the boys away to shield them from seeing.

SMASHER. Alright, missus. No need to get yourself fussed. Got a bob for the skull off of a feller in Sydney. To measure and that. Got to boil it up real good first. Nice and clean.

LOVEDAY. Pickling... Pickling. Better than boiling. For the scientific... (*Misses the word, tries again.*) For the scientific gentleman. Pickling retains a greater degree of data.

SMASHER hangs the ears on his belt.

SMASHER. For good luck like.

BLACKWOOD moves across the room toward him.

What?... What!

BLACKWOOD seizes SMASHER in a headlock and punches him three times in the face until SMASHER drops to the floor.

BLACKWOOD. You damn little maggot.

BLACKWOOD takes one last look at SMASHER and then is out the door.

DAN and BIRTLES move to help him.

SMASHER. Fuck off!

He looks up through his bloodied face.

That bugger'll be sorry he done that.

They all leave except SAL and THORNHILL.

SAL. We maybe better go, Will.

THORNHILL. Go where, where have we got to go?

SAL. Home.

THORNHILL. We ain't got enough. Nowhere near!

SAL. How much then, Will? How much is enough? Better poor than dead.

THORNHILL. That's where we disagree, Sal.

Beat.

SAL. I don't want that Smasher Sullivan showing his face here no
    more.

Scene Fourteen

Darkey Creek.

DHIRRUMBIN. One blue and silver morning a week after the
    attack at Twist's, *The Hope* glided past the place known as
    Darkey Creek. It was an absence that Thornhill noticed. For
    once there was no smoke rising out of the gully. As he stepped
    out to wade ashore, he felt the silence deepen.

    THORNHILL *enters.*

    A few humpies around the coals of a dead fire. A couple of
    empty flour bags in the dirt, a bark dish where a damper had
    been mixed, the scraps dry and tinged with green. And then he
    saw them.

THORNHILL. Oh, please God, no.

DHIRRUMBIN. Figures curled on the ground like lumps of
    gnarled wood. A man, a woman, arched in death, mouths ajar.

    *He backs away, not wanting to see this, when he hears a soft
    groaning.*

THORNHILL. Jesus God.

DHIRRUMBIN. And there was a child. A boy. Still alive.

    *The boy lies with his knees drawn to his chest, his face sticky
    with dried vomit.*

    He arches his body in a spasm.

    THORNHILL *kneels down and takes the boy in his arms.*

    He was surprised at the softness of the boy's black hair… and
    under it he felt the shape of his skull, the same as his own son's.

    The boy looks up. Their eyes meet.

THORNHILL. Ain't nothing I can do for you, lad.

THORNHILL *remains holding the boy.*

DHIRRUMBIN. He wanted to go, to leave this place, to let someone else find it. But the boy would not stop looking at him so he held him in the silence, wanting a sound, a bird's call, the wind in the trees, anything, but even the mosquitoes had abandoned the place.

He knew he would never share with Sal the picture of this boy. It was another thing he was going to lock away in the closed room in his memory, where he could pretend it did not exist.

Scene Fifteen

The River Flat.

The corn stands tall… the cobs ripe for picking. BURYIA, GILYAGAN, NARRABI *and* GARRAWAY *are among the patch, picking it, laughing, calling out to each other, filling their dillybags up.*

WILLIE *comes down from the hut.*

WILLIE. Oi… get out of it!… Da… Da… the blacks are taking the corn. Da!

THORNHILL *and* DAN *come running down from the hut,* SAL, DICK *and* MRS HERRING *soon after.*

THORNHILL. Get out of it!

He runs into the corn, takes BURYIA *by an arm and drags her away. The old woman kicks out at him as* GILYAGAN *fights him off with a stick. He feels it come down hard across his head. He lets* BURYIA *go to seize the stick from* GILYAGAN's *grasp. He snaps it in two and strikes her hard across the face. She falls.* BURYIA *is on his back now, shrieking, scratching, kicking. He slaps her hard. He kicks her hard.* NARRABI *attacks* THORNHILL *and is belted across the face.*

SAL. Jesus, Will… enough!

DICK *is frozen. Stiff with shock.*

NGALAMALUM *and* WANGARRA *have arrived.*

WANGARRA. Narrabi, Buryia ngalbung nung! [*Go now!*]

THORNHILL. No take our tucker, you black bastards.

WILLIE *has fetched the gun.*

WILLIE. Da, Da.

SAL. No, Willie.

THORNHILL *seizes the gun and points it at them.*

The women and NARRABI *crawl away to meet the men.*
WANGARRA *helps* BURYIA *and they slip back into the
forest. All except* NGALAMALUM, *who holds his ground,
daring* THORNHILL *to shoot.*

THORNHILL. Fuck off! Or I'll shoot you, Jack.

MRS HERRING. Don't.

THORNHILL. I'm asking you to depart in a civil manner.

But NGALAMALUM *does not turn.* THORNHILL *closes his
eyes and feels his finger tighten on the trigger. At the last
moment he points it to the sky and fires. The recoil a solid punch
to his shoulder. A curl of blue smoke in the air.*

NGALAMALUM *stands his ground and then slowly walks
away.*

DAN (*entering with* GARRAWAY). I got one here.

GARRAWAY. Biyal, biyal, biyal! [*No, no, no!*]

DICK. Garraway.

He twists and fights the white man off until DAN *twists his
arm high behind his back to make him still. On the boy's leg a
flap of skin hangs down bright red.*

DAN. Tie him up like bait. Shoot the others when they come to
get him. Smasher done it that way.

SAL. Let him go, Dan... Can't be no good come out of this.

DAN. Are you going to let them walk all over you, man?

SAL (*approaching to do the job herself*). For God's sake, Will, let him go.

DAN *waits for the word from* THORNHILL.

THORNHILL. Let him go.

DAN *releases his grip. And spits. It lands close enough to* THORNHILL'*s boots to tell him what he thinks.*

GARRAWAY *takes a few steps, his arm is broken from* DAN'*s twisting. It hangs lose by his side. He staggers. He stands still. Unable to move forward or back.*

DICK. Go... go, will ya.

GARRAWAY *walks again but this time he falls.* DICK *goes to help, his father reaches for him, but the boy shakes him off. He lifts* GARRAWAY *to his feet, hugging him to do so.*

Please, Garraway... Warrawa. Warrawa.

GARRAWAY *takes a few more steps until the bush absorbs him. He looks back at his friend... both boys knowing that it will never be the same between them.*

They are all silent. Stunned.

THORNHILL. They'da taken the lot. Six months' work.

SAL *gives no sign that she heard.* THORNHILL *goes to say it again.*

They'd taken –

SAL. I heard you the first time, Will.

MRS HERRING *walks forward and picks up a cob of corn.*

MRS HERRING. Best get what's left.

Slowly, they each start to pick the remaining corn.

DHIRRUMBIN. That night they went to bed early. But no one slept. Thornhill sat at the door, the gun loaded. Ready to kill a man.

By morning Sal had become a woman turned to wood. Even in their worst days in London, with Thornhill in Newgate Prison waiting to die, she had not gone into herself like this. And then she made a decision. Without looking at him, she walked off along the track that led to the other side of the point. He tried to stop her but she would not be stopped. She had never been this far from their hut. Never wanted to. But she had to see something for herself. Their place.

Scene Sixteen

The Dharug Camp.

SAL *moves within the Dharug camp… the domestic arrangement of the camp still in place but now it is empty of people; the humpy, the mixing bowls, the grinding stones, even the broom made of rushes. Nothing had been taken.*

SAL. They've gone.

   THORNHILL *enters.*

THORNHILL. Best come away, pet.

   She takes up the broom and starts to sweep. The patch is as clean swept as her own yard.

Best leave it.

   She stands uselessly with the broom still in her hands.

SAL. They was here… Like you and me was in London. Just the exact same way. You never told me. You never said. Their grannies. And their great-grannies. All along. Even got a broom to keep it clean, Will. Just like I got myself.

THORNHILL. Why ain't they here then, if they reckon it's their place?

SAL. They are here. Out there. This very minute. They ain't going nowhere. They got nowhere else to go.

THORNHILL. We had to go. Wasn't our choice. Now it's them that has to.

She says nothing.

It's just a hundred acres, Sal. They got all that.

She says nothing.

Seven years old I was when I first pulled an oar.

SAL. I know that. No one's worked harder than you.

THORNHILL. And what have I got to show for it? Nothing. I ain't never owned nothing. And with no way to move up in the world. But now I own this.

SAL. Who says you own it? Where's the piece of paper that says that?

THORNHILL. I don't need no paper.

SAL. We best leave. While we still got the chance. Today.

THORNHILL. We ain't going nowhere.

SAL. I can have us packed in an hour. Be miles away by dinnertime.

THORNHILL. They ain't never done a hand's turn. They got no rights to any of this. No more than a sparrow.

SAL. That's as may be but we're going. Back to Sydney. Or up to Windsor if you want. Until we've got enough to get us home.

THORNHILL. Home! I don't know that home any more. A house in Swan Lane and a couple of wherries ain't enough any more.

SAL. Don't say that.

THORNHILL. Your songs and your stories. The names of your streets. They don't mean nothing. Not to me, not to your sons.

SAL. No.

THORNHILL (*mocking her in song*). 'Oranges and lemons, say the bells of St Clement's...' We were nothing in London. Nothing to London. Place spat us out like it spat all them others out.

SAL. No! It spat you out, Will Thornhill. I chose to come here. With you. For you. And I can choose to go back. With my boys.

THORNHILL. Damn you!

He raises his hand to strike her. She does not flinch.

SAL. Hit me if you want. But it won't change nothing.

He lowers his arm. In that moment his life was a skiff with no oar, caught on the tide. Until they hear DAN *running down toward them. He enters, heaving for breath.*

DAN. They set fire to Sagitty's. I seen the smoke from down the point.

SAL. That's it.

SAL *is the first to move.*

THORNHILL. Look, Sal –

SAL (*cutting him off*). You go and help Sagitty. The minute you get back we're on our way. With or without you, take your pick.

Scene Seventeen

Sagitty Birtles' Place.

In a clearing still smouldering from fire and spread with broken plates, BIRTLES *stands pinned to a tree with a spear in his guts, blinking with the shock of it. His shirt is blood-soaked. He holds the spear steady with one hand and in the other he holds a china teacup.*

BIRTLES. Came at sun-up, Will.

As THORNHILL *and* DAN *enter…*

Broke me plates. All of them. But not me best china cup… Take it, will you?

THORNHILL. Save your strength, Sagitty.

BIRTLES. Take it, man. It's all that's left.

THORNHILL *takes the cup.*

Will… I don't want to die.

THORNHILL. You won't, matey. We'll get you up to Windsor.

DAN. He ain't got a chance.

THORNHILL. We're going to get him up to Windsor.

DAN *takes hold of the end of the spear and holds it steady as* THORNHILL *slips the saw blade between* BIRTLES' *back and the tree.*

BIRTLES. Oh, Jesus God.

THORNHILL *starts to saw, and with each thrust,* BIRTLES *screams in agony.*

Scene Eighteen

The Maid of the River.

DHIRRUMBIN. The tide was with them, Windsor no more than a couple of hours away. Sagitty lying – in the slops of water in the bottom of the boat.

Thornhill knew there would be no keeping this from Sal. He thought of her back at the hut. Making ready to leave the place without a backward glance. In no time at all it would be as if the Thornhills had never called it theirs. He could not bear it. The loss. Of this place he'd dared to call his own.

THORNHILL, DAN, LOVEDAY *and* SMASHER *are silent as they pass a bottle of rum between them at the bar of The Maid of the River.*

They carried Sagitty up to the hospital. He was out of sight, but Windsor was just two dusty streets and a wharf, and from the bar of The Maid of the River they could hear the man's screams as the spear was pulled from his belly.

In the silence that followed, they did not need to be told that he was dead.

Word travelled fast and by mid-afternoon the place was full. Men came from Sackville and South Creek, from Richmond and beyond.

Smasher Sullivan made the story his own, as if he was there himself. If he told it once he told it fifty times. And with each telling and with each new round of rum the details of it grew. Of how – they stuck old Sagitty with a spear...

SMASHER. They stuck old Sagitty with a spear like he was an insect on display in a glass case and they made him watch as they slit the throat of his dog and left it at the end of the chain. Every fucking plate in the hut was smashed, each tin cup flattened, each spade broken and each piece of furniture made into splinters and the whole lot burned along with his field of wheat and corn.

DHIRRUMBIN. Thornhill drank and said nothing. Maybe it was the noise of the place, the sound of men's voices or maybe just the rum playing with his mind.

TURNKEY. William Thornhill.

THORNHILL. That's my name.

DHIRRUMBIN. But it seemed that for a moment he was back in the crowded cell in Newgate Prison among the moans and cries of men condemned.

TURNKEY. William Thornhill.

THORNHILL. That's my name.

DHIRRUMBIN. And he thought of every man who had ever stood over him. Judges and gentlemen. Governors and captains.

TURNKEY. William Thornhill.

THORNHILL. THAT'S MY NAME!

TURNKEY. We are graciously pleased to extend our grace and mercy unto him.

THORNHILL. I can't hear you.

TURNKEY. And grant him our pardon for his said crime on condition of his being transported to the Eastern Part of New South Wales for the term of his natural life.

THORNHILL. I can't hear you.

TURNKEY. You're to live, you miserable sod. Life, man. It's yours. Take it.

SMASHER. We got to deal with them. Get them before they get us.

DHIRRUMBIN. And then he was back in the crowded bar of The Maid of the River. With the smell of rum and sweat and fear filling the room.

SMASHER. Only one here with the guts enough to say what we all want. Ain't none left up at Darkey Creek. Sagitty saw to that, rest his soul. But there's a whole bleeding camp of them up at Blackwood's.

DHIRRUMBIN. He felt something inside him slow down.

SMASHER. We can get there tonight. Settle the lot of them by breakfast.

DHIRRUMBIN. He stared into his glass of liquor.

SMASHER. Only thing is we got to have *The Hope* to get us up there.

DHIRRUMBIN. He felt the eyes of the room on him. And Dan whispering hot in his ear.

DAN. Get rid of 'em and Sal will stay, Will. Ain't no other way to hold her.

LOVEDAY. We must grasp the nettle, painful though it may be, or else abandon the place to the treacherous savages and return to our former lives.

SMASHER (*reading him*). Nobody won't ever know, I swear. Not even our wives.

DHIRRUMBIN. It's like a knot in old rope. Hard as a fist. No point trying to tease it out. Just a matter of getting hold of a good sharp knife and cutting it.

THORNHILL *drinks off the rest of his glass.*

THORNHILL. Tonight then.

DHIRRUMBIN. They were nineten men when *The Hope* left
Windsor. It was dark by the time they reached the First Branch.
There they tied up and waited for the dawn tide to take them up
to Blackwood's Lagoon.

Thornhill sat on the stern deck. He watched over these waiting
men and wondered how they had come to this. He tried to
make it in his mind that he had no choice in this but each way
he looked at it there was no backing away. The choice was his
and he was making it.

An hour before dawn he felt the tide shift under the keel. He
put his weight on the tiller and slowly the tide grew stronger
than the river and pushed *The Hope* toward the lagoon.

SMASHER. Get the men first. Then we clean up the breeders.

DHIRRUMBIN. In the first dim light, they slid over the side and
waded to shore. Nothing moved as they approached the camp.

Until the birds lifted from the trees at the sound of the first
gunshot.

*In voices low and trembling the men start to sing as they
advance forward, their guns raised... puffs of smoke rising
with each shot. We almost can't pick it in their rough voices
until slowly it becomes clear and builds... as what we knew to
be a nursery rhyme becomes a terrifying song of war.*

MEN (*singing*).
London Bridge is falling down,
Falling down, falling down.
London Bridge is falling down,
My fair lady.

Build it up with wood and clay,
Wood and clay, wood and clay,
Build it up with wood and clay,
My fair lady.

Wood and clay will wash away,
Wash away, wash away,
Wood and clay will wash away,
My fair lady.

Build it up with bricks and mortar,
Bricks and mortar, bricks and mortar,
Build it up with bricks and mortar,
My fair lady.

Bricks and mortar will not stay,
Will not stay, will not stay,
Bricks and mortar will not stay,
My fair lady.

Build it up with iron and steel,
Iron and steel, iron and steel,
Build it up with iron and steel,
My fair lady.

Scene Nineteen

The Thornhills' Hut.

SAL *is seated by the light of a lamp.* WILLIE *and* DICK *have fallen asleep at her side. Their belongings are packed, ready to go.*

THORNHILL *enters. He cannot look at his sons. She searches his face.*

SAL. Sagitty?

THORNHILL *shakes his head.*

THORNHILL. There won't be no more trouble. They've moved on for good now. No need for us to go nowhere.

SAL. I hope you ain't done nothing. On account of me pushing at you.

THORNHILL. Nothing's been done.

The boys wake.

DICK. Is Garraway alright? Da… and Narrabi?

THORNHILL *is silent. And in that terrible silence the truth is seen.*

DICK *leaves the hut.*

SAL. Don't go off, Dick.

THORNHILL. Let him go. We won't speak of this again.

SAL. Is that it, Will? What we have now. Me and you? Silence?

End of Act Two.

Epilogue

1824.

The Dharug enter… one by one… each throwing a handful of dirt over their shoulder as they fall.

DHIRRUMBIN. The old woman Buryia was the first to be shot. And then Gilyagan, and other women and their children. And then the men. Narrabi tried to run. A bullet in his knee made him fall. Loveday finished the job with a club of wood. Garraway was taken by a man's sword. The back of his head sliced away. Wangarra got a spear up. But Dan got him with a shot in the back. The spear fell, unthrown. Tom Blackwood came running down from his hut, shocked from his sleep and screaming with rage. Smasher took him down with his whip. One to his face, which took an eye. And with him lying on the ground, blinded, they continued the job. Yalamundi, the old man, stood and watched as people fell. He tried to lift the club at his waist. But it was as if his strength had been taken. And then he saw him; the one who had come. Thornhill. He didn't know why he had come. Or why he had stayed so long. He thought that if they waited long enough he would leave their place.

THORNHILL *and* YALAMUNDI *stand facing each other across the battlefield.*

Thornhill saw the old man and raised the gun. It went off with a puff of blue smoke. He thought he must have missed for the old man was still standing there, with a question on his face. Thornhill thought to answer, if he knew the meaning of the question being asked, before the old man's legs collapsed beneath him and he sat politely down in the dust. Blood came from his mouth, just a trickle like spit but so red. And then he lay down and kissed the earth with the blood from his mouth.

And a great shocked silence hung over the lagoon.

It took them the day to burn the bodies. They saw the smoke from Windsor. Just a farmer burning the cleared timber from his block, they thought.

NGALAMALUM *enters, ten years older now. He takes a place at the fire.*

Ngalamalum survived. A shot from Smasher's gun had not quite killed him. The place on the side of his head where bone and skin had been blasted away could still be seen. It had bound itself back together lumpily. The shot had done other damage too, that left one leg dragging and something wooden about his face so that it showed nothing: no pleasure, no pain.

Someone else survived that day. The one Blackwood called his wife, Dulla Dyin. At the sound of the first shot she took her child and sheltered in the bushes where she watched the slaughter unfold. She wanted to turn away. She wanted to run. But she made herself watch. She knew that someone had to see this.

SAL *enters, ten years older now and no longer pregnant. The child that was born that year is now in the cold earth beneath the weathered stone, which she stands before.*

THORNHILL *enters. He wears a fine coat now and a pair of new boots that gives him the walk of a man of substance.*

THORNHILL. Go in now, Sal, it's getting dark… Sal? Did you hear me?

SAL. Jack's back. Did you see?

THORNHILL. I saw the smoke down the point.

SAL. Take him down your old coat. It's turning cold.

A moment. He thinks to say something more to her. But can't find the words.

SAL *opens her hand and lets the broken piece of tile from Wapping New Stairs fall onto the grave of her dead child.*

* * *

The River Flat.

NGALAMALUM *sits by a little fire around the point. Older now. No longer the man who once held a spear to* THORNHILL'*s face in anger. Someone gone away. Here in a broken body only.*

THORNHILL *approaches, bearing his old coat.*

THORNHILL. Here, Jack, keep yourself warm.

> NGALAMALUM *makes no acknowledgement of him or the gift, which* THORNHILL *lays on the ground beside him.*

Get yerself some tucker, up the house. Missus look after yer.

He mimes eating, bringing his hand to his mouth.

I give you tucker, round the back. Cuppa tea. Plenty sugar.

NGALAMALUM *gives him nothing.*

I would, mate, honest to God. I know what it is to be hungry… What? Too good for my offer of help, are you? Then I wish you'd take your sorry black arse away from here. You lot got to learn to help yourselves now. Can't just be sitting around in the dirt all day, like bludgers.

> THORNHILL *reaches to lift him by the arm. At his touch* NGALAMALUM *comes to life.*

NGALAMALUM. NO!

He slaps the flat of his hand hard on the ground, raising the dust.

This me… My place.

The sound of water as it laps against the riverbank and of birds rising and of the wind gathering in the tops of the trees.

NGALAMALUM *remains by the fire as* DHIRRUMBIN *sings a song of mourning.*

As THORNHILL *builds his fence…*

The End.

Oranges and Lemons

from 'Secret River'

Vox

Trad

Gilyagan's Song

from 'Secret River'

Richard Green
arr:IG

If I was...

from 'Secret River'

Vox

Trad
arr. IG

Drunken, Energized ♩ = 110

I wish I was an ap-ple on an ap-ple tree an ap-ple

tree_____ You'd come by, take a bite of me_____

If I was an ap-ple on an ap - ple tree

I wish I had a brandy and a jug of beer a jug of beer
With my arms around my dear
Brandy and a jug of beer

I wish I was a king and very rich, very rich
Give it all up for one little kiss
Of your ruby red lips

Little Fish

from 'Secret River'

Trad, via Jenny Thomas
and Mel Robinson
Arranged : IG

1.There's a song in my heart for the one I love
2.The crew is a - sleep And the o - cean's at
3.The an - chor's a - weigh And the wea - ther is
4.There are fish in the sea___ There's no doubt a-

best___ And her pic - ture's tat - tooed all___ o - ver my chest___ Hey
rest;___ And I'm sing - ing this song To the ones I love best.___ Hey
fine;___ And the Cap - tain's on deck, a - waltz-ing in time.___ Hey
bout it___ Just as good as the ones That have e - ver come out of it Hey

CHORUS

[1,2,3]ho, lit - tle fish - y, Don't___ cry,___ don't___
[4]ho, lit - tle fish - y, Good___ night,___ good___

cry Hey ho,___ lit - tle fish - y, don't___ cry.___

night, Hey ho,___ lit - tle fish - y, good___ night.___

Dharug Song over the top (from Chorus 2 - repeated as necessary):
Banilung Banilung Banilung Banilung Banilung (Melody - EEE DDD CCC DDD CCC
Banilung Banilung Banilung Banilung Banilung (Melody as above etc..)
Nura-Da Nura-Da Nura-Da Nura-Da Nura-Da
Nura-Da Nura-Da Nura-Da Nura-Da Nura-Da
Guwuwi Nura-Da Nura-Da Nura-Da Nura-Da Nura-Da Nura-Da Nura-Da
Guwuwi Nura-Da Nura-Da Nura-Da Nura-Da Nura-Da Nura-Da Nura-Da

Garabari Song

from 'Secret River'

Vox

Richard Green
arr: IG

www.nickhernbooks.co.uk

 facebook.com/nickhernbooks

 twitter.com/nickhernbooks